Renae B. Humburg, Ed. D.
Vocational/Career/Federal Programs Coordinator
Laramie County School District #1
Cheyenne, Wyoming

Merle Wood
Education Consultant
Formerly of Oakland Public Schools
Lafayette, California

South-Western Publishing Co.

Developmental Editor: Jane Phelan
Production Editor: Karen Roberts
Associate Director/Design: Darren Wright
Production Artist: Sophia Renieris
Associate Photo Editor/Stylist: Kimberly A. Larson
Associate Director/Photography: Diana W. Fleming
Assistant Photographer: Mimi Ostendorf
Marketing Manager: Shelly Battenfield

Cover: Stamp design © 1991 United States Postal Service.

Copyright © 1993
by SOUTH-WESTERN PUBLISHING CO.
Cincinnati, Ohio

ALL RIGHTS RESERVED
The text of this publication, or any part thereof, may not be reproduced or transmitted in any form or by any means, electronic or mechanical, including photocopying, recording, storage in an information retrieval system, or otherwise, without the prior written permission of the publisher.

ISBN: 0-538-70774-7

1 2 3 4 5 6 7 8 9 0 DH 98 97 96 95 94 93 92
Printed in the United States of America

This book is printed on recycled, acid-free paper that meets Environmental Protection Agency standards.

▲▲▲ PREFACE

PUNCTUATION presents basic information on punctuation rules and how to apply them. This self-paced, individualized text-workbook is written specifically for the adult learner. It is designed to foster student success.

SPECIAL FEATURES

PUNCTUATION is designed specifically to help you invest in the future of your adult learners and to meet your instructional needs. Some features of the text-workbook include the following:

• A larger typeface makes the text-workbook easy for students to use and to read. Pages are colorful and uncrowded.

• Competency-based methodology is used. Clear objectives are followed by short segments of instruction. Activities immediately reinforce one or a short series of rules.

• Content and examples relate to adult-level, real-life issues and skills.

• Pretests and posttests, with answers, provide self-evaluation.

• Study breaks provide refreshing and useful information that contributes to the general literacy of the student.

• Abundant exercises enable students to experience frequent and meaningful success.

• Goals for each exercise provide motivation and direction.

• Bonus Exercises in the manual support all exercises and give the students another chance to succeed.

• Answers to all exercises facilitate independent, self-paced learning.

• Personal progress is recorded by the student after completing each exercise.

• Evaluation guides in the student's Personal Progress Record measure individual success.

INSTRUCTOR'S MANUAL

The Instructor's Manual provides instructional strategies and specific teaching suggestions for PUNCTUATION along with supplementary bonus exercises and answers, additional testing materials, and a Certificate of Completion.

Bonus Exercises. A bonus exercise, matching each exercise in the text-workbook, is provided in the manual. These bonus exercises give students a second chance to reach the goals set for each exercise. Answers to the bonus exercises are in the manual. These materials may be reproduced for classroom use.

Testing Materials. Two additional tests in the manual allow for more flexible instruction and evaluation.

Certificate of Completion. Upon completion of PUNCTUATION, a student's success may be recognized through a Certificate of Completion. This certificate lists the skills and topics covered in this text-workbook. A certificate master is in the manual.

CONTENTS

GETTING ACQUAINTED vii
HOW YOU WILL LEARN vii
WHAT YOU WILL LEARN vii
SPECIAL FEATURES viii
READY TO START ix

CHECKING WHAT YOU KNOW x

UNIT 1   ENDING PUNCTUATION MARKS 1
WHAT YOU WILL LEARN 1
INTRODUCTION TO PUNCTUATION 1
PERIOD 2
QUESTION MARK 4
EXCLAMATION POINT 5
WHAT YOU HAVE LEARNED 6
PUTTING IT TOGETHER 7

UNIT 2   COMMAS THAT SEPARATE 9
WHAT YOU WILL LEARN 9
WHY USE COMMAS? 9
COMMAS THAT SEPARATE ITEMS IN A SERIES 9
COMMAS THAT SEPARATE PARTS OF
  ADDRESSES AND DATES 11
WHAT YOU HAVE LEARNED 13
PUTTING IT TOGETHER 14

UNIT 3   COMMAS THAT CONNECT COMPLETE THOUGHTS 16
WHAT YOU WILL LEARN 16
RECOGNIZING SIMPLE SENTENCES 16
RECOGNIZING COMPOUND SENTENCES 21
PUNCTUATING COMPOUND SENTENCES 22
WHAT YOU HAVE LEARNED 23
PUTTING IT TOGETHER 24

UNIT 4   COMMAS THAT SET ASIDE 27
WHAT YOU WILL LEARN 27
WORDS THAT INTRODUCE 27
WORDS THAT INTERRUPT 30
WHAT YOU HAVE LEARNED 36
PUTTING IT TOGETHER 37

UNIT 5   APOSTROPHE AND DIRECT QUOTATIONS 40
WHAT YOU WILL LEARN 40
THE APOSTROPHE 40
QUOTATION MARKS 47
WHAT YOU HAVE LEARNED 49
PUTTING IT TOGETHER 50

UNIT 6   COLON AND SEMICOLON 53
WHAT YOU WILL LEARN 53
THE COLON 53

THE SEMICOLON 57
WHAT YOU HAVE LEARNED 62
PUTTING IT TOGETHER 63

CHECKING WHAT YOU LEARNED 66

GLOSSARY 69

INDEX 71

ANSWERS 75

PERSONAL PROGRESS RECORD 82

GETTING ACQUAINTED

You frequently must write notes, memos, and letters. Punctuation skills are needed for both personal and job use.

The purpose of writing is to communicate with the reader. Punctuation marks make writing easier to understand. Each punctuation mark is a signal or sign that helps the reader along the way.

HOW YOU WILL LEARN

PUNCTUATION will help you improve your writing skills. You will learn to use punctuation marks quickly and easily.

Learn at Your Own Pace

You will progress through this book on your own. If you move ahead faster, or go slower, than other students don't be concerned. You are to work at *your* best speed.

Learn Skills Successfully

Learning objectives and goals for each unit will tell you what you are to accomplish. You will study a topic, then you will complete an exercise. This lets you practice what you have just learned. When you have shown that you know the topic, you will move on to the next topic. If you have not learned the topic, you will do more practice exercises. You will know how well you are doing as you move through each step in this book.

Complete Bonus Activities

You may not reach your goal on every practice activity. When this happens, you should review the lesson and then do a bonus exercise. The bonus exercises cover the same material as the practice exercises. They give you a second chance to reach your goal. Your instructor has copies of the bonus exercises.

Check Your Own Success

You will keep track of your own success. You will check all of your answers in the back of this book. Then you will record your scores on your own Personal Progress Record.

WHAT YOU WILL LEARN

Your ability to punctuate correctly is important to your writing skill. As you study PUNCTUATION, you will learn to punctuate successfully using the following marks: period, question mark, exclamation point, comma, apostrophe, quotation marks, colon, and semicolon. You will know the basic rules for punctuation and be able to use them in your writing. To achieve these goals you will study six units:

Unit 1 Ending Punctuation Marks
Unit 2 Commas That Separate
Unit 3 Commas That Connect Complete Thoughts
Unit 4 Commas That Set Aside
Unit 5 Apostrophe and Direct Quotations
Unit 6 Colon and Semicolon

SPECIAL FEATURES

PUNCTUATION has a number of special features that will help you learn and apply the material successfully.

Checking What You Know

You can check what you already know before starting this book. Checking What You Know lets you know what skills you need to improve. After completing the book, you will do Checking What You Learned. By comparing the two scores, you will see how much you've learned.

Checkpoints and Activities

Each unit has several practice exercises. Each Checkpoint immediately applies the rules you have just learned. Putting It Together applies and reinforces the skills you learned in the unit.

Bonus Exercises

If you do not reach the goal for any of the Checkpoints or Putting It Together activities, you should review the unit. Then do the Bonus Exercise. This bonus work gives you a second chance to succeed. Your instructor has copies of these bonus exercises for you. Your instructor also has the answer key to these activities. You will use it to check your own work.

Answers

Answers to all the exercises appear in the back of this book. The color-tinted pages make the answers easy to find and use. Always do the exercise *before* you look at the answers. Use the answers as a tool to check your work—not as a means of completing the exercise.

Personal Progress Record

After checking your work, you will record your score on your Personal Progress Record. It is found in the back of this book.

After you complete a unit, you will know your level of success.

Certificate of Completion

When you finish this book, you may be eligible for a Certificate of Completion. Your instructor will explain to you the skill level required for this award.

READY TO START

You are now ready to start improving your ability to use punctuation marks in your writing. When you finish, you should be able to apply the punctuation rules in your writing.

Your new skills benefit you. You can write with added confidence. You will have improved career opportunities in the world of work where, in many cases, well-developed written communications skills are required.

Turn to page x and complete Checking What You Know. Check your answers with the answers on page 75. Then begin Unit 1, Ending Punctuation Marks.

CHECKING WHAT YOU KNOW

Take this pretest before starting PUNCTUATION. The test will show you how well you can use punctuation marks and the skills you should improve.
   There is no time limit, so take your time. When you finish, check your answers. Give yourself 2 points for each correct answer. Record your score on the Personal Progress Record on page 82. After finishing the book, you will be able to see how much you learned.

INSTRUCTIONS: Select the sentence that is correctly punctuated. Place the letter of the correct answer in the blank.

- __a__ 0. (a) Her name is Mrs. J. L. Nelson.
          (b) Her name is Mrs J. L. Nelson.

Unit 1

_____ 1. (a) Jose Romero, M D, is a medical doctor.
         (b) Jose Romero, M. D., is a medical doctor.
_____ 2. (a) Please clean up after dinner.
         (b) Please clean up after dinner?
_____ 3. (a) Will you please tell me where you work?
         (b) Will you please tell me where you work.
_____ 4. (a) Where do you work?
         (b) Where do you work.

Unit 2

_____ 5. (a) They ordered lumber, and plumbing supplies.
         (b) They ordered lumber and plumbing supplies.
_____ 6. (a) She lives in Torrington, Wyoming, near the park.
         (b) She lives in Torrington, Wyoming near the park.
_____ 7. (a) He lives in Apt. 2 444 Allen Road, Lawrence KS, 66044-5094.
         (b) He lives in Apt. 2, 444 Allen Road, Lawrence, KS 66044-5094.
_____ 8. (a) The last reunion was held in March, 1990.
         (b) The last reunion was held in March 1990.

Unit 3

_____ 9. (a) Ann heard the instructions but did not understand the assignment.
         (b) Ann heard the instructions, but did not understand the assignment.
_____ 10. (a) The child climbed the fence and played with the dogs.
          (b) The child climbed the fence, and played with the dogs.
_____ 11. (a) Joe has to learn how to drive heavy equipment, or he will not get the job at the coal mine.
          (b) Joe has to learn how to drive heavy equipment or he will not get the job at the coal mine.

PUNCTUATION

Checking What You Know   xi

_____ 12. (a) The discount store will be open every night, but the shopping center will close early on Sundays.
(b) The discount store will be open every night but the shopping center will close, early on Sundays.

Unit 4

_____ 13. (a) Yes I will be happy to write a letter recommending you for a job.
(b) Yes, I will be happy to write a letter recommending you for a job.

_____ 14. (a) While Joe was in Seattle, his aunt took care of his son.
(b) While Joe was in Seattle his aunt took care of his son.

_____ 15. (a) She will buy new clothes, after she gets her paycheck.
(b) She will buy new clothes after she gets her paycheck.

_____ 16. (a) The order, however, has not been received.
(b) The order however has not been received.

_____ 17. (a) They called the person who manages the trailer court to report the broken window.
(b) They called the person, who manages the trailer court, to report the broken window.

_____ 18. (a) Jolene Davis the office manager will send you a letter.
(b) Jolene Davis, the office manager, will send you a letter.

_____ 19. (a) Josie, I hope you will send me the package next week.
(b) Josie I hope, you will send me, the package next week.

Unit 5

_____ 20. (a) The company is celebrating it's first year in business.
(b) The company is celebrating its first year in business.

_____ 21. (a) He delivered todays' paper.
(b) He delivered today's paper.

_____ 22. (a) They lost their driver's licences in the auto accident.
(b) They lost their drivers' licences in the auto accident.

_____ 23. (a) His mother's and father's native language is French.
(b) His mother and father's native language is French.

_____ 24. (a) Roy said that Joe would call the unemployment office today.
(b) Roy said that, "Joe would call the unemployment office today."

_____ 25. (a) They were assigned to read Chapter 5, "Careers in Construction."
(b) They were assigned to read Chapter 5, <u>Careers in Construction.</u>

Unit 6

_____ 26. (a) They loaded the following items into the truck: two chairs, one bed, and three desks.
(b) They loaded the following items into the truck two chairs, one bed, and three desks.

_____ 27. Business letter salutation:
(a) Dear Ms. Davis:
(b) Dear Ms. Davis,

_____ 28. (a) Mary cleared the table; and Joe washed the dishes.

(b) Mary cleared the table; Joe washed the dishes.

_____ 29. (a) Joe works late on Saturdays; however, he goes to work at 6:30 a.m. on Sundays.

(b) Joe works late on Saturdays, however, he goes to work at 6 30 a.m. on Sundays.

_____ 30. (a) The company has offices in the following cities: Pierre, South Dakota, Billings, Montana, and Pullman, Washington.

(b) The company has offices in the following cities: Pierre, South Dakota; Billings, Montana; and Pullman, Washington.

☞ **Check your answers on page 75. Record your score on page 82.**

UNIT 1

Ending Punctuation Marks

WHAT YOU WILL LEARN

When you finish this unit you will be able to:
- Identify the three ending punctuation marks.
- Use the correct punctuation mark to end sentences.
- Use the period correctly in ending initials and abbreviations.

INTRODUCTION TO PUNCTUATION

The purpose of writing is to communicate with the reader. Punctuation marks are used to make writing easier to understand. Each punctuation mark is a signal or sign that helps the reader along the way.

You see signals every day. You know that a green light means "go." A red light means "stop." When you drive a car, you signal when you want to turn. In ball games, the umpire signals "time out."

Illustration 1-1

Signals tell you to take notice.

Ending punctuation marks are also signals. They tell you when you are at the end of a sentence. The ending mark tells you to pause briefly and then read on. If you are reading sentences out loud, you should pause at the end of each sentence. The ending marks are:

Period .
Question Mark ?
Exclamation Point !

PERIOD

Rule Use a period at the end of a sentence. A sentence is one word or a group of words that expresses a complete idea. The period stops the sentence. It tells the reader to pause. The period tells the reader that a complete idea has been stated.

Four kinds of sentences end with periods.

- Statement—Jane works at a bank.
- Command—Meet me at the bank.
- Request—Please meet me at the bank.
- Polite request—Will you please deliver these items.

A polite request often sounds like a question. If you expect someone to *act* rather than to *answer,* the sentence is a request.

Rule Use a period after the initials of a person's name. The initial letter of a person's name is the first letter.

The initials for Don Allen Martinez are: D. A. Martinez

Rule Use a period after abbreviations. **Abbreviations** are shortened forms of words.

Abbreviated titles before a name: Mr. Dan Adams, Mrs. Rose Garcia, and Dr. Jane Chang attended the reception.
Abbreviated titles after a name: Joe Mendoza, Sr., is the father of Joe Mendoza, Jr.
Sr. is an abbreviation for senior.
Jr. is an abbreviation for junior.
Jane Gregorio, M.D., is a medical doctor.
Mike Chong, D.D.S., is a doctor of dental surgery or a dentist.

Rule Use a period after time periods.

The bus left at 8:30 a.m. and returned at 9:00 p.m.

Rule Street addresses and names of the days and months should be spelled out. Abbreviate the word "apartment" in sentences if it is followed by a number.

The baby was born on Monday, August 2.

Unit 1   Ending Punctuation Marks   3

DID YOU KNOW?

OK is a slang term that means "all right" or "correct."

Sometimes OK is written O.K. This word is pronounced "okay." OK is used by millions of people from around the world. Many American movies and TV shows are shown in other countries. Many of these films include the word OK.

People have tried to trace the first time OK was used. No one knows for sure what the letters "O" and "K" mean. Some people say that OK came from the initials of the Old Kinderhook Club. The club supported Martin Van Buren for president in 1840. Van Buren's nickname was Kinderhook Fox.

Radio operators used OK for the term "all correct." They responded with OK to tell the sender that they had received the message. Others think that people simply liked the sound of OK. OK is now accepted as a word.

He lives at 942 North Oak Avenue.
Her address is Apt. 405, 112 South Fifth Street.

Rule   Some abbreviations do not use periods. Examples are names of government agencies and words that are commonly used.

CD	Compact Disc
FBI	Federal Bureau of Investigation
TV	Television
UN	United Nations
USA	United States of America

CHECKPOINT 1–1

YOUR GOAL:
Insert correctly 15 or more ending marks.

Proofread each sentence. Insert periods in the proper places in each sentence. The first one has been completed as an example.

• His name is Mr. J. L. Allen.

1. Will you please move your truck

2. Her name is Mrs R S Barnes

3. She took the baby to Dr Chris Canfield

4. Work starts at 7:30 a m

5. He bought a videotape for his VCR set

6. His address is Apt 202, 110 Main Street

7. Her new title is Mary Meza, M D

8. He sent the money to Alan Davis, Jr , and Jake Jones, Sr

9. They bought a used TV set

10. Please send me the letter

☞ *Check your work on page 75. Record your score on page 82.*

DID YOU KNOW?

The ending punctuation mark period comes from *periodos* which means "a going round" in Greek. The end of a sentence most often requires a period. This marks the end of a cycle or circle. The symbol for a period is a round dot. In other words, the period rounds out or completes the sentence.

QUESTION MARK

Use a question mark at the end of a sentence that asks a direct question.

Direct question: When is he going home?

Do not confuse an indirect question and a direct question. A direct question reports someone else's question. Use a period after an indirect question.

Indirect question: Please tell me when he is going home.

CHECKPOINT 1–2

YOUR GOAL: Insert correctly 4 or more ending marks.

This checkpoint reviews the rules for punctuating direct and indirect questions. In the following, insert a period or question mark at the end of each sentence. The first sentence has been completed as an example.

- Is the babysitter here yet?

1. Tell me when the babysitter is coming

2. Why do little children ask so many questions

3. The child asked her why the grass was green

4. Why is the sky blue

5. When will your mother be home

☞ *Check your work on page 75. Record your score on page 82.*

DID YOU KNOW?

Have you ever tried to speak to someone who did not understand your language? Do you use sign language? You probably do. When you want to say goodbye, you wave. When you want to tell someone you are pleased, you nod your head up and down and smile.

Some people do not hear spoken language. A hearing-impaired person may use sign language to communicate. The deaf are able to communicate in the English language. Many are good lip readers. They appreciate it when their family and friends learn to talk to them with their hands.

You will see sign language used on TV programs and in schools. Signers use their hands and arms to communicate a question mark.

In sign language a question mark is drawn in the air.

EXCLAMATION POINT

Rule Use the exclamation point at the end of a word or group of words that express strong feeling. Exclamation points add emphasis.

> Wonderful! He got the job.
> Stop the car!
> Congratulations!

Do not overuse exclamation points in business writing. Too many exclamation points cause sentences to lose emphasis.

The most exclamation points will be found in the comics. Look at a comic strip in the newspaper. Notice that many comic strip writers use exclamation points. The comic characters speak with great emotion.

CHECKPOINT 1–3

YOUR GOAL:
Insert correctly 8 or more ending marks.

In the following lines, insert an exclamation point in the proper place. The first sentence has been completed as an example.

- Congratulations on your new job!

1. I am so surprised

2. Hurry   The engine room is on fire

3. Help   There has been an accident

4. Oh   The back tire is flat

5. Slow down   The road is slippery

☞ **Check your work on page 75. Record your score on page 82.**

WHAT YOU HAVE LEARNED

As a result of completing this unit, you have:
- Identified the three ending punctuation marks.
- Applied the rules for correctly using punctuation marks at the end of sentences and in abbreviations.

PUTTING IT TOGETHER

ACTIVITY 1-1 YOUR GOAL: Insert correctly 13 or more ending marks.

In each of the following sentences, insert ending marks where they are needed. The first one is completed as an example.

- She is moving to Apt. 4 in a different building.

1. Will her son be going to school next year
2. She attended a parenting class to learn how to help her son read better
3. The teacher told the parents to take their children to the public library
4. She reads to her children every evening before they go to bed
5. Will you please take Jimmy to the babysitter
6. He works nights and takes care of the baby during the day
7. Congratulations   You won the prize
8. Her next job interview will be on Monday at 3:30 p m
9. The doctor's name is Mary Chavez, M D
10. Her favorite TV program is on at 8 p m on Tuesdays

☞ **Check your work on page 75. Record your score on page 82.**

ACTIVITY 1-2 YOUR GOAL: Insert correctly 9 or more ending marks.

In each of the following sentences, insert the proper punctuation marks. Decide if the sentences are direct questions or indirect questions. The first one is completed as an example.

- He wondered when the employment office would open.

1. When will the personnel office be open
2. When will there be jobs in construction
3. She wondered where the office was located
4. What time is your job interview
5. He asked her what time the meeting was
6. What time is the meeting
7. When will they give the test

7

8. He asked them when they would be giving the test

9. His daughter wanted him to come to visit her classroom

10. What is the teacher's name

☞ **Check your work on page 75. Record your score on page 82.**

ACTIVITY 1-3 YOUR GOAL: Insert correctly 25 or more ending marks.

In each of the following sentences, insert ending marks where they are needed. The first one is completed as an example.

- Will you please return the books to the library.

1. Is your sister going to work tomorrow

2. They will send their son to a day-care center

3. Is the plumber coming to fix the sink

4. His name is Mr A C Jackson, Jr

5. Will you please move your car

6. Watch out The roads are slick

7. She goes to work at 6 a m

8. The doctor's name is Joe Sanchez, M D

9. He wondered when the reading class would be offered

10. When will the library be open

11. The child asked why the sky was blue

12. He asked them when the cattle truck would arrive

13. What time does the rodeo begin

14. The next show starts at 7:15 p m

15. He asked them to move their truck

16. Give your child a choice for lunch

17. Ask him if he wants a peanut butter sandwich or a bowl of soup

18. Will you please help me fix this sandwich

19. Where is the bread

20. Will you please clean up after lunch

☞ **Check your work on page 75. Record your score on page 82.**

UNIT 2

Commas That Separate

WHAT YOU WILL LEARN

When you finish this unit, you will be able to:
- Correctly insert commas between items in a series.
- Correctly insert commas between and after parts of an address.
- Correctly insert commas between and after parts of a date.

WHY USE COMMAS?

The comma is a punctuation mark that helps to make the meaning of the sentence clear. Commas do not end sentences. Commas separate or set aside words or groups of words within a sentence. Words follow the comma in a sentence. A comma tells the reader to pause and then go on.

When you write, you need to give the reader signals. These signals should help the reader to understand better what you are trying to say. Commas are signals. They tell you that certain words or groups of words should be separated.

Using commas correctly makes it easier for you to communicate what you want to say. The following are rules for commas that separate.

COMMAS THAT SEPARATE ITEMS IN A SERIES

A **series** contains three or more similar words or groups of words. Items in a series are placed one after another in a sentence. Notice in the examples that a comma comes before the connecting word such as *and, nor,* and *or*. The connecting word appears before the last item in the series. The items in the series are italicized.

> **Rule** Use commas to separate three or more items in a series.

> She will work *Monday*, *Tuesday*, or *Wednesday*.
> Joe uses a *computer keyboard*, *screen*, *printer*, and *telephone* in his job.

9

Unit 2 Commas That Separate

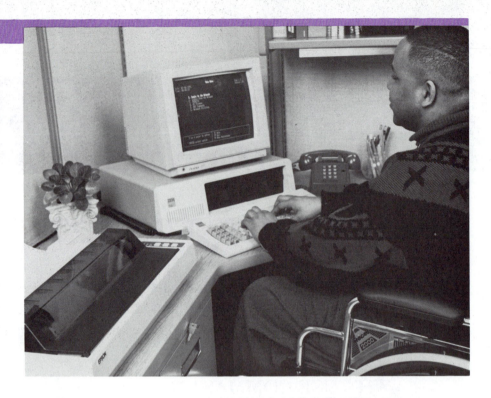

Illustration 2-1

Joe uses a computer keyboard, screen, printer, and telphone in his job.

Jack works as a waiter in a restaurant. He *sets the table*, *takes orders*, *delivers food*, and *prepares sales tickets*.
Karen works as a stock clerk in a warehouse. She *unloads the truck*, *marks the boxes*, and *places the boxes on shelves*.

✓ CHECKPOINT 2–1

YOUR GOAL: Correctly insert 25 of 28 commas.

Proofread the following sentences. Insert commas in the proper place in each sentence where they are needed. The first sentence has been completed as an example.

- She is studying math, history, and government.

1. Her children are named Billy Mike Sue and Josie.

2. After work she will stop at the day-care center the pharmacy the grocery store and the gas station.

3. He works on Monday Wednesday Thursday and Friday.

4. He took the bus through Iowa Nebraska South Dakota and Montana.

5. She would like to study to become a carpenter a plumber an electrician or a welder.

6. She is enrolled in welding and carpentry courses.

7. He hopes to complete his job training in June July August or September.

8. Their favorite sports are baseball basketball swimming and bowling.

9. The auto mechanic said that his old car needs a spare tire a battery spark plugs and a side mirror.

10. The carpenter drew a blueprint designed the table and ordered the lumber.

11. The hotel maid cleaned the floor changed the sheets and dusted the furniture.

12. He will fill out an application and write a letter.

☞ **Check your work on page 76. Record your score on page 83.**

DID YOU KNOW?

The word *comma* is derived from the Greek word *komma*. The word *komma* came from the word *koptein* which means to cut off. The comma is a punctuation mark that does cut off or separate parts of a sentence from other parts.

COMMAS THAT SEPARATE PARTS OF ADDRESSES AND DATES

Rule Use a comma to separate parts of addresses. Parts of an address that are separated include the name, street address, city, and state.

> She lives in Detroit, Michigan, one mile from the airport.
> Her son was born in Milwaukee, Wisconsin, in 1989.
> She lives at 102 Day Street, Sedalia, Missouri, near the park.

Rule Do not separate the ZIP Code from the state with a comma. Use the two-letter state abbreviations only when using ZIP Codes.

ZIP is an abbreviation for Zone Improvement Plan. The United States Postal Service assigns ZIP codes to all addresses. Each delivery area in the country has its own ZIP code. Use the five-digit ZIP code plus the four-digit code if it is known. The ZIP code in the following address is 53705-4218.

> He lives at 1010 Allen Avenue, Madison, WI 53705-4218.

Illustration 2-2

ZIP Code Directories are available at your local postal service office.

CHECKPOINT 2–2

YOUR GOAL:
Correctly insert 16 of 18 commas.

Proofread the following sentences. Insert commas in the proper place in each sentence. The first sentence has been completed as an example.

- He lives at 102 Park Place, Des Moines, Iowa.

1. He was born in Dallas Texas.

2. The package was sent to 102 School Street Ness City KS 67560-1290.

3. The convention was scheduled to be held in Boise Idaho after the spring holidays.

4. They live in Apt. 5 405 Fifth Street St. Paul Minnesota.

5. We celebrate our anniversary in Estes Park Colorado each year.

6. She moved to Phoenix Arizona last year.

7. The next game will be played in Las Vegas Nevada.

8. She mailed the note to Helena Montana.

9. Send the check to 112 Park Place Madison WI 53705-4100.

10. His office is at 104 Park Drive Lansing MI 48917-6782.

☞ **Check your work on page 76. Record your score on page 83.**

Unit 2   Commas That Separate

> **Rule**   Use a comma to separate parts of dates. A specific date includes the month, day, and year. Use a comma between the date and the year and after the year. Separate the day (for example, Thursday) from the date (June 14).

On Thursday, June 14, 1989, the auto plant was closed.

Commas are not required when only the month and year or month and day are given.

In January 1992 the new work stations arrived for our office.
It was on May 4 that they began to repair the highway.

✓ CHECKPOINT 2–3

YOUR GOAL: Correctly insert 10 of 12 commas.

Proofread the following sentences. Insert commas in the proper place in each sentence where they are needed. The first sentence has been completed as an example.

- The meeting will be held on September 5, 1995, in Little Rock.
1. He was born on Tuesday April 23 1991 in Canton.
2. The state law was passed on May 1 1990 in Santa Fe.
3. The convention was scheduled for May 10 1995 in Seattle after the spring holidays.
4. The family reunion was held in September 1982 at the church.
5. We celebrate our anniversary on July 10 each year.
6. He broke his leg on August 10 1976 in an auto accident.
7. The next game will be played on Thursday December 12.
8. She mailed the note on June 17 1990.
9. Send the check by August 15 next year.
10. He was born on February 6 1968.

☞ **Check your work on page 76. Record your score on page 83.**

WHAT YOU HAVE LEARNED

As a result of completing this unit, you have learned to:
- Correctly insert commas in a series.
- Correctly insert commas in an address.
- Correctly insert commas in a date.

PUTTING IT TOGETHER

ACTIVITY 2-1 YOUR GOAL: Correctly insert 13 of 15 commas.

Proofread the following sentences. Insert commas in the proper place in each sentence where they are needed. The first sentence has been completed as an example.

- The teacher speaks French, Spanish, and English.

1. He ordered nails lumber electrical wire and paint.
2. His company hired carpenters plumbers electricians and carpet installers.
3. They drove to town to pick up parts for the tractor.
4. The store sent seed catalogs to farmers and ranchers.
5. She delivered bread to bakeries grocery stores and restaurants.
6. The school janitor takes out the trash cleans the floors scrubs the walls and mows the lawn.
7. The stock clerk loads the truck and unpacks boxes.
8. The farmer raises wheat barley and corn.
9. The rancher also feeds cattle sheep and pigs.
10. The stove and sink need to be cleaned.

☞ **Check your work on page 76. Record your score on page 83.**

ACTIVITY 2-2 YOUR GOAL: Correctly insert 15 of 17 commas.

Proofread the following sentences. Insert commas in the proper place in each sentence where they are needed. The first sentence has been completed as an example.

- He lives at 555 Elgin Place, Houston, Texas.

1. He was born in Santa Barbara California.
2. The package was sent to 3720 James Street Topeka KS 66614-4445.
3. The meeting will be held in Salt Lake City Utah after the game.
4. They live in Apt. 7 709 Jay Avenue Madison Wisconsin.
5. We will celebrate her birthday in Tulsa Oklahoma this year.
6. She moved to Memphis Tennessee last year.

14

Unit 2   Commas That Separate

7. The next game will be played in Baltimore Maryland.

8. He mailed a letter to Pierre South Dakota.

9. Send the check to 402 Jason Court Cheyenne WY 82001.

10. His office is in Portland Oregon.

☞ **Check your work on page 76. Record your score on page 83.**

ACTIVITY 2-3 **YOUR GOAL:** Correctly insert 14 of 16 commas.

Proofread the following sentences. Insert commas in the proper place in each sentence where they are needed. The first sentence has been completed as an example.

- She was born on April 10, 1980, in Jackson, Mississippi.

1. He was born on May 1 1989 in Mobile Alabama.

2. They met on January 1 1990 in Miami Florida the day after his birthday.

3. The meeting was scheduled for Wednesday September 5 1998 in Atlanta Georgia following the convention.

4. They live in Apt. 5 800 Rand Road Omaha Nebraska.

5. We sent in our records on October 4 1990.

☞ **Check your work on page 76. Record your score on page 83.**

UNIT 3

Commas That Connect Complete Thoughts

WHAT YOU WILL LEARN

When you finish this unit, you will be able to:
- Identify a simple sentence.
- Identify subjects and predicates in sentences.
- Identify compound subjects and compound predicates in sentences.
- Define the term *independent clause.*
- Identify a compound sentence.
- Tell the difference between a simple sentence and a compound sentence.
- Name at least three connecting words used in joining two inde-pendent clauses in a compound sentence.
- Correctly use a comma in connecting two independent clauses in compound sentences.

RECOGNIZING SIMPLE SENTENCES

A sentence is a group of words that expresses a complete thought. Sentences that have one main idea are called **simple sentences**.

    Joe fixed dinner.
    Janice built a cabinet.

A sentence contains two basic parts—the subject and the predicate.

Simple Subjects and Predicates

The **subject** is the main word or group of words that tells who or what the sentence is about. The subject may be a single word called a noun. A **noun** is a person, place, thing, or idea that is spoken about.

Mary built the house.
John's father is a bus driver.
The auto technician repaired the car.

The subject may also be a pronoun. A **pronoun** is a word that is used in place of a noun. Pronouns that may act as subjects of the sentence include *I, you, he, she, it, they, we,* and *one*. In the second sentence the pronoun *he* takes the place of the noun *cook*.

The cook prepared the meal.
He prepared the meal.

Illustration 3-1

He is *the cook*.

These pronouns are the subjects of the sentences. The pronouns are italicized.

She also built a chair.
I work on a ranch.
He works at the hospital.
She drives a truck.
Do *they* live in town?
They live on a farm.
Park your car in the parking lot. (*you*)

In polite requests or commands the subject is *you*. Even though the word *you* does not appear in the sentence, *you* is understood to be the subject.

Please send me the application form. (The pronoun *you* is the subject.)
Call the ambulance immediately. (The pronoun *you* is the subject.)

CHECKPOINT 3–1

YOUR GOAL:
Underline 4 or more subjects correctly.

Proofread the following simple sentences. In each of the sentences underline the subject with one line. If the subject is *you* in a polite request or command, write <u>you</u> at the end of the sentence. The first one has been done as an example.

- The <u>waiter</u> set the table.

1. The young girl walked to school.

2. He rides the school bus.

3. Please serve the meal.

4. The mechanic fixed the bus.

5. Ben works in the school lunchroom.

☞ **Check your work on page 76. Record your score on page 83.**

    The **predicate** is the second part of the simple sentence. The predicate tells what the subject is or does. The predicate contains the verb and its modifiers (words that describe the verb). Verbs may show action such as *toss, run, write, walk*. The predicate is italicized in the examples.

Gary *works*.
Gary *works on a farm*.
Mary *spoke*.
Mary *spoke to her son*.

    The predicate may also tell what the subject is or has. Forms of the verb *to be* (*am, is, are, was, were*) and *to have* (*have, has, had*) express timing. They are called "helping verbs." Helping verbs are used with action verbs to show when action occurred.

	Subject	Predicate
Mike *is* tired.	Mike	is tired
The child *was* happy.	the child	was happy
Were you at the meeting?	you	were at the meeting
The office *has been* cleaned.	the office	has been cleaned

    How do you find the subject of a sentence? Look first for the predicate. Then ask the questions: *Who?* or *What?* The predicate is italicized in each sentence. The subject answers *who* or *what*.

Unit 3   Commas That Connect Complete Thoughts   19

>   Jane drove the tractor. (Who drove the tractor? *Jane*)
>   Please send me the application form. (Who should send me the application form? *You*)

To find the subject of a sentence that asks a question, change the question to a statement. The answer to the question is the subject.

>   Did you vote yesterday? (*You* did vote. *You* is the subject.)
>   Call the ambulance immediately. (Who should call the ambulance? *You*)

✓ CHECKPOINT 3–2

YOUR GOAL: Underline 9 or more subjects and predicates correctly.

Proofread the following simple sentences. In each of the sentences underline the subject with one line. If the subject is *you* in a polite request or command, write <u>you</u> at the end of the sentence. Underline the predicate with two lines. The first one has been done as an example.

- <u>Bob</u> <u><u>works</u></u>.

1. The repair person fixed the computer.
2. Joe studied his lesson.
3. Send me the bill.
4. Barbara fixed the car.
5. The leader of the group spoke.
6. Please repair the leaky sink.
7. He played softball after work.
8. Is Dan selling his bike?
9. My boss called this morning.
10. Kevin walked home.

☞ **Check your work on page 76. Record your score on page 83.**

Compound Subjects and Compound Predicates

A **compound subject** has two or more subjects in the same sentence. The subjects are connected by *and* and *or*.

DID YOU KNOW?

A compound is anything that is made by combining parts. Medicines are also compounds. They usually contain combinations of two or more chemicals. Water is a compound of two chemical elements. These elements are hydrogen and oxygen. The symbol for water is H_2O.

Teresa and Jane loaded the truck.
Eleanor and Mark repaired the broken tractor.
Bob or Kim fixed the flat tire.
The teachers and students entered the building.

A **compound predicate** has two or more predicates in the same sentence.

Joan *cut the board* and *hammered the nails*.
Jerry *cleaned the windows* and *vacuumed the carpet*.

CHECKPOINT 3–3

YOUR GOAL: Underline 9 or more subjects and predicates correctly.

Proofread the following sentences. In each of the sentences underline the subject or compound subject once. Underline the predicate or compound predicate with two lines. The first one has been done as an example.

- He cut the potatoes and cooked the stew.

1. She prepared the salad and set the table.
2. You and I will mix the cement.
3. Harold fixed the fence and repaired the tractor.
4. Josie loaded the truck and drove to the ranch.
5. Miners and equipment operators worked at night.
6. Carl and Maria will load the bricks.
7. Joe and Jake cut the wood.
8. Aunt May wrote a letter and called on the phone.
9. Nancy answered the telephone and took a message.
10. Gary climbed the fence and chased the dogs.

☞ **Check your work on page 77. Record your score on page 83.**

RECOGNIZING COMPOUND SENTENCES

When you write, you may want to join two or more simple sentences into one compound sentence. A **compound sentence** contains two or more simple sentences joined by a connecting word.

> Gina is taking swimming lessons, but she is struggling with learning to breathe correctly.
> Joe is driving to work today, and Jason is taking the bus.

A simple sentence is called an "independent clause" when it is part of a compound sentence. A **clause** is a group of related words that contain a subject and a predicate. An **independent clause** contains a subject and predicate and can stand alone as a complete sentence.

When two or more independent clauses are combined, they form one compound sentence. Short words connect the two independent clauses. The connecting words used most often are *and, but,* and *or*.

> He heard the instructions,   *but*   he did not understand them.
> (independent clause)   (independent clause)

A balance is a scale that weighs certain items. This kind of scale has been in use for hundreds of years. A pan hangs from each end of the horizontal bar of the scale. Weights are placed in both pans. When both weights are equal, the bar remains horizontal and is balanced.

Illustration 3-2

Compound sentences are balanced.

A compound sentence is like a balance scale. It has two sides that balance equal parts. These equal parts are independent clauses.

DID YOU KNOW?

A compound sentence is like a compound word. When the words *air* and *plane* are combined, they form one compound word *airplane*. When the words *air* and *port* are combined, they form one compound word *airport*.

CHECKPOINT 3–4

YOUR GOAL: Underline 9 or more independent clauses correctly.

Underline the independent clauses in the following compound sentences. Do not underline the connecting words *and, but, or*. The first one has been done as an example.

- <u>Joe went to the store</u>, and <u>Mary picked up the children at school</u>.

1. They need to fix the car, or Mary will have to walk.

2. The neighbor's dog barked, but they did not hear it.

3. Jake unloaded the truck, and Joe then sent him to the warehouse.

4. Jane loaded the wheat on the truck, and Joe took it to the grain elevator.

5. The children ride the bus to school, but they still need a ride to football games at night.

☞ **Check your work on page 77. Record your score on page 83.**

PUNCTUATING COMPOUND SENTENCES

A comma is used to separate two independent clauses in a compound sentence.

Rule Use a comma before *and, but,* and *or* when they join two independent clauses in a compound sentence.

Marty went to the hospital, but his health did not improve.
The store will deliver the TV, or Dan will pick it up.

CHECKPOINT 3–5

YOUR GOAL: Correctly punctuate 9 or more sentences.

Proofread each sentence and decide whether it is a compound sentence or a simple sentence. If it is a compound sentence, insert a comma before the connecting word. The first one has been completed as an example.

Unit 3   Commas That Connect Complete Thoughts

- Joan will complete her vocational training in June, but she will not start working until September.

1. Betty is not home from work yet and Joe is not home yet either.
2. The book report was finished last week and will be turned in today.
3. The book report was finished last week and the book will be returned to the library today.
4. Joe went to the store to buy food and will return in an hour.
5. Joe went to the store to buy groceries and Jane stayed home to take care of the baby.
6. He works at a cattle feedlot and goes to school one night a week.
7. He is working at a feedlot during the day but he still finds time to go to school at night.
8. The keyboarding course will be held two nights a week but the math course will not be held until next month.
9. Joan filled out the job application and took it to the employment office.
10. Joe filled out the job application and he made an appointment for an interview.

☞ **Check your work on page 77. Record your score on page 83.**

WHAT YOU HAVE LEARNED

As a result of completing this unit, you have learned to:
- Recognize a simple sentence.
- Recognize compound subjects in simple sentences.
- Recognize compound predicates in simple sentences.
- Recognize independent clauses in a compound sentence.
- Identify a compound sentence.
- Describe the difference between a simple sentence and a compound sentence.
- Correctly use a comma in a compound sentence that connects two independent clauses.

PUTTING IT TOGETHER

ACTIVITY 3-1 YOUR GOAL: Underline 9 or more subjects correctly.

Proofread the following sentences. Underline the subjects with one line. Some sentences have compound subjects. The first one has been done as an example.

- <u>The cook</u> fried the hamburgers.

1. His brother and sister walked to the bus stop.
2. Did the teacher correct the tests?
3. Mary and Adam work at the meat-packing plant.
4. Please send me the package.
5. She works in the sheriff's office.
6. Please pick up the spare parts.
7. Will Danny and Pat be at work today?
8. Jarvis and Kim will move to Seattle next month.
9. Diane loaded the cattle feed on the truck.
10. Her mother is learning to speak English.

☞ **Check your work on page 77. Record your score on page 83.**

ACTIVITY 3-2 YOUR GOAL: Underline 9 or more predicates correctly.

Proofread the following simple sentences. Underline the predicates with one line. Some sentences have compound predicates. The first one has been done as an example.

- She <u>loaded the truck</u> and <u>drove to the landfill</u>.

1. She changed the flat tire.
2. Has he paid the rent?
3. The dog barked.
4. The boy chased the dog.
5. They cleared the table and loaded the dishwasher.
6. Please clean your room and take out the trash.
7. Margaret installed the dishwasher.

Unit 3   Commas That Connect Complete Thoughts

8. He washed and ironed the clothes.

9. Jerry rode the horse.

10. Joan cut the wood and loaded the truck.

☞ **Check your work on page 77. Record your score on page 83.**

ACTIVITY 3-3 YOUR GOAL: Identify 9 or more subjects and predicates correctly.

Proofread the following sentences. Identify the sentences as simple sentences or compound sentences. Place an S in the space to the left if the sentence is a simple sentence. Place a C in the space to the left if the sentence is a compound sentence. The first one has been done as an example.

- __C__   He won the rodeo prize on Saturday, and he was injured on Sunday.

1. _____ The sales persons and cashiers went home.

2. _____ My car was hit by another car, but I was not hurt.

3. _____ Jane heard the CD player and turned it off.

4. _____ Joe heard the knock at the door, but he did not answer it.

5. _____ Mary and Teresa work at the truck stop.

6. _____ George takes the bus to work, or his sister drives him to work.

7. _____ Marcy and Terry are going to vocational school.

8. _____ They go to school in the morning and work at night.

9. _____ Mary took care of the children today, and Joe shopped for the groceries.

10. _____ Jane vacuumed the halls and washed the laundry.

☞ **Check your work on page 77. Record your score on page 83.**

ACTIVITY 3-4 YOUR GOAL: Correctly punctuate 18 or more sentences.

Proofread the following sentences. Some of these sentences are compound sentences. They should include a comma to separate the two complete thoughts. Other sentences do not need commas. Insert the comma where needed. The first one has been completed as an example.

- Dan finishes his computer class in May, and he hopes to have a new job in June.

1. Jerry was late for work yesterday but he worked late today.

2. The highway was finished last week and will be open to traffic today.

3. Her apartment was finished last week but she will not move yet.

4. Mary went to work and will be home tonight.

5. Jason went to the store to buy baby food and bread.

6. He works at a gas station but he would rather work on a ranch.

7. Linda drove to the vocational school and she enrolled in a welding course.

8. The airplane mechanic checked the plane and wrote a safety report.

9. Jane likes being a waitress but she does not like working at night.

10. The mechanic checked the tires and installed a new battery.

11. Juanita will have to learn how to operate the tractor or she will not get the job.

12. He told the story about the accident but his friends would not listen.

13. She works at the truck stop at night but she did not quit her day job at the garage.

14. He fixed the motorcycle for Dan and then left for home.

15. Jane works in the warehouse but she would rather work in the bus garage.

16. He grabbed the little dog and the cat climbed the tree.

17. Carrie went to the doctor and I went to see my counselor at school.

18. She liked her part-time job and hopes to go back to work after the baby is born.

19. Main Street is the busiest street in town but it is filled with potholes.

20. My sister was at the farm all day but she refused to help with the chores.

☞ **Check your work on page 77. Record your score on page 83.**

UNIT 4

Commas That Set Aside

WHAT YOU WILL LEARN

When you finish this unit, you will be able to:
- Use commas correctly after introductory words, phrases, and clauses.
- Describe the difference between a dependent clause and an independent clause.
- Use commas correctly to set aside nonessential words, phrases, and clauses in sentences.
- Use commas correctly to set aside appositives in sentences.
- Use commas correctly to set aside names in direct address.

WORDS THAT INTRODUCE

Most sentences follow a certain order. The subject is placed first. The predicate comes later.

   He drove the car.
   She lives in Chicago.
   They visit the factory.

You may want to change the sentences to make your writing more interesting. Words may be added to introduce the main idea of the sentence.

DID YOU KNOW?

You introduce yourself when you meet someone for the first time. You introduce yourself when you interview for a job. Usually, you say your name and shake hands with the person who is interviewing you.

27

Introductory Words and Phrases

Words that come before the main idea of the sentence are said to introduce the sentence. Remember, the main idea is also called the independent clause. Generally, a comma separates the introductory word or words from the main idea of the sentence.

Compare the following sentence to those on page 27. Notice the introductory words.

Yes, he drove the car.
By the way, she lives in Chicago.
Whenever possible, they visit the factory.

Rule Use a comma after a word that introduces the main idea of the sentence.

Read the following sentences out loud. Pause after each comma. Pausing after each comma may help you to understand the rule.

Finally, (pause) she found a job she liked.
No, (pause) I will be leaving soon.
Well, (pause) I hope you will be attending the meeting.

Rule Use a comma after a phrase that introduces the main idea of the sentence. A **phrase** is a short group of words. A phrase does not contain a subject and a predicate.

Read each sentence out loud. Pause after each comma. Then continue reading. Pausing after each comma may help you to understand the rule. The comma follows the phrase that introduces the main idea of the sentence.

For example, (pause) I would like to work on a ranch.
In conclusion, (pause) we hope that you send us the report.
In short, (pause) I like living in a small town.

Words or short phrases that answer the question, "When?" are usually not separated with a comma.

When are you leaving?

On Friday I will leave.
Yesterday I left for town.
Tomorrow we will go.

CHECKPOINT 4–1

YOUR GOAL: Correctly punctuate 9 or more sentences.

This checkpoint is a review of the rules for using the comma after introductory words and phrases. Proofread each sentence and insert a comma in the proper place. The first sentence has been completed as an example.

Unit 4   Commas That Set Aside

- By the way, she is trying to do what is best for her family.
1. Finally the baby next door stopped crying.
2. As a result Joe Chan was able to sleep.
3. Therefore it is time to go to bed.
4. First I want the best day-care center for my child.
5. However I want to find a good job.
6. On the other hand I do want to spend more time with my son.
7. For example I don't want to work at night.
8. Also I need to find an apartment to rent.
9. Fortunately my mother can babysit for me.
10. In addition she will help clean my apartment.

☞ **Check your work on page 78. Record your score on page 83.**

Introductory Clauses

Clauses also introduce sentences. Remember, a clause is a group of words that includes both a subject and a predicate. A clause that introduces the independent clause (main idea) is an **introductory clause**. Unlike an independent clause, an introductory clause does not tell a complete thought. Introductory clauses cannot stand alone. They are called *dependent clauses* because they depend on the rest of the sentence for meaning.

Some words are commonly used in introductory clauses. If you become familiar with them, you will be able to recognize introductory clauses more easily.

after	before
although	if
as	since
because	when

Rule   Use a comma after an introductory clause that introduces the main idea of the sentence.

Read each sentence out loud and pause where marked.

After he arrived, (pause) it started to rain.
As you can see, (pause) the mobile home park is close to school.
Because of the weather, (pause) the roads were closed.
Before he left, (pause) he checked with the highway patrol.
If you learn how to use commas, (pause) your writing will improve.

Since the weather changed, (pause) the picnic was called off.
When she called, (pause) the line was busy.

Dependent clauses also end sentences. When they appear at the end of a sentence, however, no commas are needed.

She will be angry *if I do not go.*
She was gone *when he arrived.*
They unloaded the goods *after the truck arrived.*

CHECKPOINT 4–2

YOUR GOAL: Correctly punctuate 9 or more sentences.

This checkpoint reviews introductory clauses. Proofread each sentence and insert a comma in the proper place. The first sentence has been completed as an example.

- After the game was over, they took the bus home.

1. If the goods are not there Bianca will drive the truck back to the store.
2. Because the boxes were stacked too high there was an accident.
3. While the carpenter worked on the cabinets the plumber installed the sink.
4. Because he decided to work late he missed the bus.
5. Since the weather changed the farmers have been happy.
6. After he went to work the day-care center called.
7. If his son is ill he will need to take off work.
8. After he drove the truck to town he stopped to pick up the machine parts.
9. She will get a raise when she completes the computer course.
10. Joe answered the phone after he heard it ring twice.

☞ **Check your work on page 78. Record your score on page 83.**

WORDS THAT INTERRUPT

What does it mean to interrupt? You are interrupted as you carry out your daily work. The telephone interrupts you at work. For example, you might be keying data on the computer. The phone rings. You stop keying to answer the phone. Your keyboard work is interrupted. After the phone call, you go back to work on the computer.

Unit 4   Commas That Set Aside

Illustration 4-1
We set aside our work tasks to handle interruptions.

Nonessential Words and Phrases

Often words are inserted in sentences that interrupt the main idea. Not all words in a sentence are needed to tell what you really mean. Words that are not important to the meaning of the sentence are **nonessential words**. The following nonessential words are italicized. These words are not necessary to the meaning of the sentences. Nonessential words are also called **parenthetical expressions.**

Sanjay is going, *by the way*, to the family reunion.
His sister, *of course*, will also be there.
Their mother, *however*, will not be able to be there.

Interrupting Words	Interrupting Phrases
consequently	after all
however	as you know
therefore	for example
unfortunately	by all means
	in my opinion
	needless to say
	of course

Rule   Use commas to set aside words or phrases that interrupt the sentence.

The order, *however*, was not filled today.
You are, *on the other hand*, well suited for this work.
The truck drivers, *of course*, will be invited to the meeting.

DID YOU KNOW?

What does it mean to set aside? You move things to one side as you work. For example, an auto technician sets aside some of her tools while she is working on a car. Not all of the extra tools are needed to fix the car.

CHECKPOINT 4-3

YOUR GOAL: Correctly punctuate 9 or more sentences.

This checkpoint reviews words and phrases that interrupt the sentence. Proofread the sentences and insert a comma in the proper place. The first sentence has been completed as an example.

- Linh Tan will, however, need to fill out a job application.

1. The meeting of course is open to the public.
2. The Trang family unfortunately will not be able to attend.
3. We will therefore visit their apartment.
4. Sonny Chan by all means deserves good pay.
5. Gina in my opinion is a very good worker.
6. The dock workers on the other hand will service the ship.
7. Painters of course will be hired to help them.
8. The fishing crew however will want to board the ship soon.
9. The next trip for example will be in the Gulf of Mexico.
10. The hurricane warnings of course are going to change plans.

☞ **Check your work on page 78. Record your score on page 83.**

Nonessential Clauses
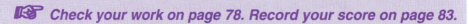

Clauses may also interrupt the main idea of the sentence. Clauses that are not important to the meaning of the sentence are **nonessential clauses.** These clauses explain or describe a person, place, or thing in the sentence. If you leave out the clause, however, the meaning of the sentence does not change. Sometimes nonessential clauses are called *nonrestrictive clauses.*

Rule Use a comma to set aside nonessential clauses in sentences.

Read the following sentences with the clauses. Then reread the sentences without the clauses. Note that in each sentence the clause is not necessary to the meaning of the sentence.

> Jan James, *who has been with the company three years*, will receive more pay. (The clause is not necessary to identify Jan James.)
> Dana, *who is a meatcutter apprentice*, will work for the Davis Country Market. (The clause is not necessary to identify Dana.)
> The Martinez Apartment Building, *which is located near the airport*, will be torn down. (The clause is not necessary to identify the Martinez Building.)

Sometimes a clause is essential to the meaning of the sentence. Without the clause, the sentence would not say the same thing. **Essential clauses** are also called *restrictive clauses.* Essential clauses are not set aside by commas. The essential clauses are italicized in the examples.

> Joe is the only member of the family *who works on a ranch.* (The clause is necessary to identify the family member.)
> The woman *who spoke to me* is my supervisor. (The clause is necessary to identify the woman.)
> The truck *that Joe drives* belongs to the company. (The clause is necessary to identify which truck belongs to the company.)

CHECKPOINT 4–4

YOUR GOAL: Correctly punctuate 9 or more sentences.

This checkpoint is a review of the rules for using the comma to set aside nonessential clauses. In the following sentences, insert a comma in the proper place. The first sentence has been completed as an example.

• Kim Anderson, who has worked in this office for two years, will help you.

1. The only computer that needs repair is in the business office.

2. Jackie De la Cruz who is the electronics technician will fix your CD player.

3. Sanjay the new student in our class moved here from India.

4. Cheyenne the capital city of Wyoming is in the southeastern part of the state.

5. Kotoe Tsuji who lives next to our mobile home is a police officer.

6. Jana is the only worker in the office who is going to school.

7. Sonny Allison who is Lisa's brother works for the highway patrol.

8. The man who lives upstairs is my brother.

9. Manuel Simental who is a police officer lives in our mobile home park.

☞ **Check your work on page 78. Record your score on page 83.**

Appositives

Appositives are words or groups of words that give additional information about a person, place, or thing. Appositives are nonessential. If you leave out the appositive, the meaning of the sentence remains the same.

> **Rule** Use a comma to set aside an appositive in a sentence.

Mr. Garcia, *the school secretary*, will help the children get on the school bus.
Eva Washington, *the head custodian*, will be checking your work.
Mike Fernandez, *the office receptionist*, was promoted to data entry supervisor.

Sometimes an appositive is necessary to identify the person, place, or thing it describes. An appositive that is essential to the meaning of the word is not set off by commas.

Her sister Erika is the babysitter. (*Erika* is needed to identify the babysitter.)
Your friend Hilario was here to see you. (*Hilario* is needed to identify which friend.)

Direct Address

When you address people, you are writing or speaking to them. When you address them directly, you use their names. People's names used in direct address interrupt sentences.

Unit 4   Commas That Set Aside

Jose, please come here.
I don't know, *Lory*, where the keys are.
Have you seen my new sweater, *Dad*?

Rule   Use commas to set aside names of people who are being directly addressed.

Read the following sentences out loud. Pause after the comma.

Mr. Quyen, (pause) I would like to make an appointment for next week.
I am not sure, (pause) *Bianca*, (pause) if the apartment is available to rent.
Pedro, (pause) your interview is set for tomorrow.

CHECKPOINT 4–5

YOUR GOAL: Correctly punctuate 9 or more sentences.

This checkpoint is a review of the rules for using the comma to set aside appositives and nouns of direct address. In the following sentences, insert commas in the proper places. The first sentence has been completed as an example.

- Carrie Flores, manager of the beauty shop, will hire more beauticians.

1. Joe Peters the security guard will open the door.

2. Jason Alford my sister's boyfriend will be our boss at the plant.

3. The next shipment Mr. Quyen will be delivered to the warehouse.

4. The next manager will be Jane Castro a computer expert.

5. Donna Robb the owner of the company will be offering bonuses to the workers.

6. I hope Ms. Rollans that you will be able to attend.

7. Kim you are invited to the party.

8. Hugo Thompson the chief of police will investigate the case.

9. John Cousins the school nurse checked their ears.

10. Uncle Bob the oldest member of the family invited the neighbors to the picnic.

☞ **Check your work on page 78. Record your score on page 83.**

WHAT YOU HAVE LEARNED

As a result of completing this unit, you have learned how to:
- Use commas correctly after introductory words, phrases, and clauses.
- Describe the difference between a dependent clause and an independent clause.
- Use commas correctly to set aside nonessential words, phrases, and clauses in sentences.
- Use commas correctly to set aside appositives in sentences.
- Use commas correctly to set aside names in direct address.

PUTTING IT TOGETHER

ACTIVITY 4-1 **YOUR GOAL:** Correctly punctuate 18 or more sentences.

This activity is a review of the rules for using the comma after introductory words. Proofread the sentences and insert commas in the proper places. The first sentence has been completed as an example.

- After they arrived, they filled out application forms.

1. For example the car has a flat tire.
2. On the other hand we could take the bus.
3. Apparently he has gone to work.
4. Because you have completed the computer course you are ready to apply for a better job.
5. Since the mail was early Mr. Epstein was able to write the report for his boss.
6. No she will not be delivering the mail.
7. While Maria fixed the engine the customer waited in the office.
8. Although he worked hard he did not come to work on time every day.
9. If he improves in math he will be able to get a better job.
10. First I want to find quality care for my child.
11. If you improve your keying speed you will receive an increase in pay.
12. In addition the bus stops near the center.
13. If Tim Kunz moves to town he will work at the meat-packing plant.
14. After Sam fed the sheep he drove to town to get groceries.
15. When the bus stops at the next corner it is time to leave.
16. After they finished eating dinner they washed the dishes.
17. In addition they swept the kitchen floor.
18. After the grain elevator closes they will drive back to the farm.
19. He stopped to pick up the tractor parts after he ate lunch.
20. While she was at work the storm blew down the power lines.

☞ **Check your work on page 78. Record your score on page 83.**

ACTIVITY 4-2   YOUR GOAL: Correctly punctuate 18 or more sentences.

This activity reviews the rules for using the comma to set aside nonessential interrupting words, phrases, and clauses; appositives; and nouns of direct address. Proofread the sentences and insert commas in the proper places. The first sentence has been completed as an example.

- Shihjeng Na, who was hired by the supervisor, is a good worker.

1. The car which has cost very little to repair is ten years old.
2. Karen who was the leader of the group turned in her report.
3. Melvin Carr the carpet installer will call to set up a time to visit.
4. Dave my neighbor's brother will take care of the baby.
5. Maria Beltran a nursing assistant delivered the food.
6. Please Mrs. Downey deliver this to the kitchen.
7. Painters of course will be hired to help them.
8. The fishing crew however will soon want to board the ship.
9. The next trip for example will be in the Gulf of Mexico.
10. Jake Ellis who has worked in this office for two days will help you.
11. The Jason Mobile Home Park which is near the highway is opening a day-care center.
12. Marie Gilkey who is the new teacher will meet with parents.
13. The Chavez Apartment Building the largest apartment building in town is located near the shopping center.
14. Alan please call me tomorrow.
15. I hope Mr. Chan that you will come back to see us.
16. You will of course come back.
17. Manuel my neighbor's brother is working at the shopping center.
18. Please Mr. Torres deliver the flowers to the hospital.
19. Josephine Henry who works at the Shear Design Beauty Salon will cut my hair.
20. My sister will help me of course when I need a babysitter.

☞ **Check your work on page 78. Record your score on page 83.**

Unit 4 Commas That Set Aside

ACTIVITY 4-3 YOUR GOAL: Correctly punctuate 15 or more lines.

Commas have been omitted from the sentences in the following paragraphs. Add punctuation in the space provided. The first sentence has been completed as an example.

- If you are looking for a job, you need to learn how to make a good impression in the job interview.

1. Before you interview for a job you should be prepared to make
2. a good first impression. Of course your clothing jewelry hair style
3. and grooming should reflect a professional image. Different jobs by
4. the way have certain standards for proper dress and grooming.
5. Consequently you need to learn about these standards.

6. When you prepare for the interview you should learn as much as
7. you can about the specific business that interests you. By all means
8. you should arrive a few minutes before the interview.

9. When you meet the interviewer listen carefully for his or her
10. name. Once the discussion begins listen carefully for questions.
11. Before you answer a question think carefully about your answer. Speak
12. clearly however when you do respond. In addition maintain eye contact
13. with the interviewer during the interview. Needless to say be sure
14. that the employer is aware of your strong points.

15. You may not have liked the last place where you worked.
16. Nevertheless you should not complain about your former employer.
17. In conclusion be prepared to make a good first impression.

☞ **Check you work on page 79. Record your score on page 83.**

UNIT 5

Apostrophe and Direct Quotations

WHAT YOU WILL LEARN

When you finish this unit, you will be able to:
- Use an apostrophe to form contractions.
- Use an apostrophe to form possessive nouns.
- Identify a direct quotation and an indirect quotation.
- Use quotation marks correctly in direct quotations.

THE APOSTROPHE

The apostrophe is used to show that letters have been omitted from a word and to show ownership of something. The proper use of the apostrophe will help your writing to be clear and understandable.

Contractions

When you contract something, you make it smaller. A **contraction** is a shorter way of writing two words. The apostrophe indicates that there is a letter missing.

	Contraction
are not	aren't
will not	won't

Rule Use an apostrophe to show that one or more letters have been omitted in a contraction.

The following are some groups of words that can become contractions.

are not	aren't
cannot	can't
could not	couldn't
do not	don't
there is	there's
will not	won't

Pronouns also form contractions. A pronoun is a word used in place of a noun. Some pronouns are: *I, you, he, she, it, we, you,* and *they*.

I am	I'm
I have	I've
you are	you're
he is	he's
she is	she's
it is	it's
we are	we're
we have	we've
they will	they'll

CHECKPOINT 5-1

YOUR GOAL: Get 9 or more sentences correct.

Proofread the sentences and insert an apostrophe in the proper place. The first sentence has been completed as an example.

• You're invited to a party.

1. Im hoping youll be able to attend.
2. Theyll be there on time.
3. Hes planning to bring the children.
4. Its supposed to be on Friday.
5. Were hoping Aunt Emily will be there.
6. Shell start work on Monday.
7. Gunther wont be there.
8. He doesnt have time this weekend.
9. Ive invited the family.
10. Claudia cant get off work this weekend.

☞ Check your work on page 79. Record your score on page 83.

DID YOU KNOW?

The word **contract** is also a noun. A contract is an agreement between two or more people. It can be enforced by law. You enter into different kinds of contracts. You may enter into an agreement to rent an apartment. Marriage is also a contract.

A **contractor** is a person who agrees to do something for another person. A building contractor is a person who agrees to build something for another person. Contractors also build roads and highways.

Possession

When you possess something, you own it. You probably have certain papers that prove that you own something. For example, you may have the title to a car. You may also have a sales receipt. The sales receipt is a piece of paper that proves you purchased items. Most receipts are printed by a cash register.

Illustration 5-1

If you want to return an item and get your money back, you need to show the clerk your sales receipt. This proves that you own the item.

An apostrophe shows **possession** or ownership. The apostrophe may also show a relationship.

This is my brother's pen. (ownership)
Dan's sister is here. (relationship)

The apostrophe shortens sentences. What would happen if there were no apostrophes? Sentences would be longer.

Instead of: the child's toy
You might write: the toy of the child

Singular Nouns

A singular noun is one person, one thing, or one place. Singular nouns that show ownership or show a relationship are said to be *possessive*.

Rule Use an apostrophe to show that a singular noun is possessive. Add an apostrophe and an *s* ('s) to the singular noun.

The first group of possessive nouns shows that something belongs to one person or to one thing. The apostrophe in the second group of possessive nouns shows a relationship between the two.

Unit 5 Apostrophe and Direct Quotations

Singular Noun	Possessive Singular Noun	
	Ownership	
child	child's toy	*(toy of the child)*
carpenter	carpenter's saw	*(saw of the carpenter)*
desk	Eric's desk	*(desk of Eric)*
	Relationship	
child	Aunt Jane's child	*(child of Aunt Jane)*
daughter	Paul's daughter	*(daughter of Paul)*
sister	Dan's sister	*(sister of Dan)*
son	Charles's son	*(son of Charles)*
	Length of Time	
month	month's pay	*(pay of a month)*
today	today's paper	*(paper of today)*
year	year's delay	*(delay of a year)*

Illustration 5-2

The father and son are related to each other. They are family relatives.

CHECKPOINT 5–2

YOUR GOAL: Get 5 correct.

Proofread the sentences and insert an apostrophe in the proper place. The first sentence has been completed as an example.

- He will take a week's vacation.

1. This is a students pencil.

2. She gave him the plumbers tool kit.

3. Josie is Dans daughter.

4. He borrowed Uncle Bens car.

5. She reported to Robertas workstation.

☞ **Check your work on page 79. Record your score on page 83.**

Plural Nouns

The plural form of a noun refers to more than one. Most nouns form their plurals by adding *s*.

Singular Noun	Plural Noun
apartment	apartments
park	parks
pencil	pencils

Rule To make a plural noun show possession, write the noun in its plural form. If the plural ends in *s*, add only an apostrophe.

Plural Noun	Possessive Plural Noun	
students	students' decision	*(decision of the students)*
two weeks	two weeks' vacation	*(vacation of two weeks)*
workers	workers' rights	*(rights of the workers)*

A few nouns do not form their plurals by adding an *s*. Instead, the spelling is changed.

The steps for forming a possessive noun are a little different for these words.

Singular Noun	Plural Noun
child	children
foot	feet
man	men
mouse	mice
tooth	teeth
woman	women

Rule To make a plural noun show possession, write the noun in its plural form. If the plural form does not end in *s*, add an apostrophe and *s*.

children	children's toys	*(toys of the children)*
men	men's clothing	*(clothing of the men)*
women	women's books	*(books of the women)*

Unit 5　Apostrophe and Direct Quotations　　45

CHECKPOINT 5–3

YOUR GOAL: Get 9 or more correct.

The following phrases include plural nouns that show possession or relationship. Rewrite the phrases so that they use an apostrophe to show possession. The first one has been done as an example.

- desks of the secretaries　　the secretaries' desks
1. tools of the carpenters　　_____
2. cars of the drivers　　_____
3. computers of the workers　　_____
4. weapons of the soldiers　　_____
5. licenses of the drivers　　_____
6. clothing of the men　　_____
7. delay of two hours　　_____
8. duties of the officers　　_____
9. books of the teachers　　_____
10. names of the women　　_____

☞ *Check your work on page 79. Record your score on page 83.*

Joint Ownership

Sometimes two or more persons may own the same item. This is called **joint ownership**. The couple in Illustration 5-3 own the car jointly.

Rule　Use an apostrophe to show that a noun with two or more owners is possessive. Add an apostrophe and an *s* ('s) to the last name only to show joint ownership.

　　My mother and father's native language is Spanish. (*the language of my mother and father*)
　　It was Mike and Jan's first apartment. (*the apartment of Mike and Jan*)
　　Jolene and Jason's truck needs a new engine. (*the truck of Jolene and Jason*)

Possessive Pronouns

Certain pronouns always show possession. The possessive pronouns include:

Illustration 5-3

This is Kim and David's new car.

my, mine
your, yours
our, ours
his, her, its
their, theirs

Rule Never use an apostrophe to spell possessive pronouns.

The pencil is *yours*. (not *your's*)
The book is *hers*. (not *her's*)
The cat cleaned *its* paws. (not *it's*)
The house is *ours*. (not *our's*)
The house is *theirs*. (not *their's*)

Some possessive pronouns are sometimes confused with contractions that sound the same.

its
it's
their
they're
your
you're

Correct   The cat cleaned its paws.

Incorrect The cat cleaned it's paws.

Correct   You're invited to the party.

Incorrect Your invited to the party.

Correct   They're going to the game.

Incorrect Their going to the game.

Unit 5 Apostrophe and Direct Quotations   47

CHECKPOINT 5–4

YOUR GOAL:
Get 9 or more correct.

Proofread the following sentences. Possessive pronouns and contractions are enclosed in parentheses ( ). Underline the word that is spelled correctly. The first one has been completed as an example.

- (Their) (<u>They're</u>) going to visit the hospital.

1. The company celebrated (it's) (its) first year in business.
2. (You're) (Your) invited to the party.
3. The book is (hers) (her's).
4. (Its) (It's) time to check the equipment.
5. This is (Carla and Pat's) (Carla and Pats) apartment.
6. The dog is (theirs)(there's).
7. The prize is (your's) (yours).
8. The book is (ours)(our's).
9. The CD player is (their's) (there's) (theirs).
10. I hope (they're) (their) at work on time.

☛ **Check your work on page 79. Record your score on page 83.**

QUOTATION MARKS

Quotation marks look like two apostrophes. They always come in pairs. They mark the beginning and ending of a word or group of words.

She said, "It is time for your interview."
She read the article titled "Saving Money."

Direct Quotation

A **direct quotation** contains the exact words that someone says. Direct quotations are rarely used in business writing.

Rule   Use quotation marks at the beginning and at the end of a direct quotation. Begin the quotation with a capital letter. Place the period inside the ending quotation mark. A comma is used to introduce the quotation.

Ruth said, "I will attend the meeting." (direct quotation)
"I am applying for a job," she said. (direct quotation)

Do not put quotation marks around an indirect quotation. The indirect quotation reports what another person said.

> Ruth said that Mark would attend the meeting. (indirect quotation)

Rule Use a comma to introduce a direct quotation. Always place a period or comma inside the ending quotation mark (.") (,").

> Pete said, "I will be leaving today."
> Dan said, "I hope you have a good trip."
> "I will be leaving today," Pete said.

Sometimes direct quotations are divided in two parts. The quotation is divided by words such as *he said, she replied, he asked.*

Rule Use quotation marks before and after each part of a divided quotation. The words that divide the quotation are set aside by commas. Begin the first word of the quotation with a capital letter. Begin the second part with a small letter unless some other rule requires a capital letter.

> "I hope," she said, "*you* will be able to attend the meeting."
> "Well," he replied, "*I'm* not sure."

CHECKPOINT 5–5

YOUR GOAL: Get 9 or more correct.

Proofread the sentences and insert quotation marks in the proper places. The first one has been done as an example.

- Jerry said, "I want to be a secretary."

1. Earl asked, Do you know how to keyboard?
2. Miriam said that she wanted to be a construction worker.
3. Bruce said, I will take an English course.
4. Marilyn replied, You will need to sign up now.
5. Doug asked Louise if she knew how to keyboard.
6. Nathan replied, I will drive to Tampa tonight.
7. I will drive to Lincoln tomorrow, Jack said.
8. Marty said, I read the newspaper this morning.
9. I hope, he said, that the delivery truck arrives on time.
10. The loading dock, she said, is located near the railroad track.

☞ **Check your work on page 79. Record your score on page 83.**

Unit 5   Apostrophe and Direct Quotations   49

Titles of Short Works and Parts of Complete Works

Rule Use quotation marks to set off short works and parts of complete works. These parts include the titles of short stories, articles within magazines, songs, short poems, chapters of a book.

Book chapter	"Build Your Strengths"
Song	"Moon Melody"
Magazine article	"Writing for Success"
Newspaper article	"Dear Abby"

Complete works such as books and magazines are underlined or written in all capital letters.

Good Housekeeping	GOOD HOUSEKEEPING
Denver Post	DENVER POST

CHECKPOINT 5–6

YOUR GOAL: Get 5 correct.

In the following sentences insert punctuation marks in the proper place. The first one has been done as an example.

- She read the newspaper article called "Major Sports Events."

1. They will sing God Bless America at the concert.
2. What's News? is my favorite section of the paper.
3. The magazine article was titled Time to Buy.
4. She read the short story titled Hearts and Flowers.
5. Be sure to read the opening chapter, Know Your Computer.

 Check your work on page 79. Record your score on page 83.

WHAT YOU HAVE LEARNED

As a result of completing this unit, you have learned how to correctly:
- Use an apostrophe to form contractions.
- Use an apostrophe to form possessive nouns.
- Identify a direct quotation and an indirect quotation.
- Punctuate direct quotations correctly.
- Use quotation marks to set off title of short works and parts of complete works.

PUTTING IT TOGETHER

ACTIVITY 5-1 **YOUR GOAL:** Get 18 or more correct.

Proofread the following sentences. Find the words that require an apostrophe. In the column to the left, rewrite the correct form of the words with the apostrophe in the correct place. If no apostrophe is needed, write *none*. The first one is completed as an example.

<u>drivers'</u> • They revoked three drivers licenses.

_____ 1. They arent going to work today.

_____ 2. This is Dales workstation.

_____ 3. The company didnt send the goods.

_____ 4. That is Mr. Garcias pen.

_____ 5. Im hoping they will be here soon.

_____ 6. He delivered todays paper.

_____ 7. Lets try to find them.

_____ 8. They wont return our calls.

_____ 9. The school celebrated its first year in the new building.

_____ 10. There will be two weeks delay in delivery.

_____ 11. She read this weeks issue of the magazine.

_____ 12. Its time to visit the doctor.

_____ 13. They will be buying ladies clothing.

_____ 14. They have a stack of the companys application forms.

_____ 15. They visited the workers coffee lounge during break.

_____ 16. We shouldnt have to wait.

_____ 17. This is David and Kevins office.

_____ 18. This is the childrens room.

_____ 19. The choice is yours.

_____ 20. I hope youre planning to apply for the job.

☞ **Check your work on page 79. Record your score on page 83.**

Unit 5   Apostrophe and Direct Quotations   51

ACTIVITY 5-2 YOUR GOAL: Get 9 or more correct.

Proofread the sentences. Insert quotation marks in the proper places. The first sentence has been completed as an example.

- He asked, "Where is the employment office?"

1. She read the newspaper article called Tips for Parents.
2. The receptionist replied, The office is located on the second floor.
3. Mary said that Joe would be starting work today.
4. They will read the poem, Snowbound.
5. Mary said that Joe will start work today.
6. The next meeting, he announced, will be on Monday night.
7. The book chapter was titled Business Letters.
8. The magazine article was titled Best Food Buys.
9. Akeo said, I would like to go back to school.
10. The idea is good, he said, but I need time to read your report.

☞ **Check your work on page 80. Record your score on page 83.**

ACTIVITY 5-3 YOUR GOAL: Get 16 or more lines correct.

Proofread the following personal letter. Quotation marks and apostrophes have been omitted from it. Place quotation marks and apostrophes in the proper places.

```
    Dear Josie,

 1. I told you Id write before our next family reunion.
 2. Arent you glad I didnt forget? Danny keeps reminding me,
 3. Mom, why havent you written to Aunt Josie?

 4. Uncle Kenny called last night. Im getting too old, he
 5. said, to wait so long for another reunion. He sent me a
 6. copy of a newspaper article titled Families and Memories.
 7. Im enclosing a copy.

 8. Were busy planning the family dinner. Im hoping Janes
 9. family will be there. Ive heard from Jakes sister. She
10. called and said, If you decide to have another reunion, be
11. sure to send the invitation to Robertas new address.
```

12. Roberta called last night and asked, What's happening?
13. I havent heard from you for over a year.

14. I replied, Im sorry. I lost your address.

15. I sent her the familys address list today.

16. Theres a chance shell be there. I hope to see you at
17. Dan and Marlenes anniversary party in May. Please send
18. me Judys new address.

   Sincerely,

   Ruth

☞ *Check your work on page 80. Record your score on page 83.*

UNIT 6

Colon and Semicolon

WHAT YOU WILL LEARN

When you finish this unit, you will be able to:
- Use a colon to introduce a list of items, an example, or an explanation.
- Use a colon to separate hour and minutes.
- Describe how to punctuate the salutation of a business letter using a colon.
- Use a semicolon to join clauses in a compound sentence.
- Use a semicolon before transitional words or phrases in a compound sentence.
- Use a semicolon between items in a series.

THE COLON

Use the colon (:) to tell the reader, "Notice what follows." Whatever follows the colon explains what came before the colon.

> He will order the following items for the office: pencils, pens, notebooks, paper, and computer disks.

The colon (:) is followed by two blank spaces. When you are keying, you strike the space bar twice after the colon.

Illustration 6-1

Notice: This person is ordering supplies.

After *The Following*

Rule Use a colon to introduce a list of items, an example, or an explanation that follows words such as *the following* or *as follows*.

> The following awards were presented to the students: attendance, honor roll, and citizenship.
> You will need the following items: computer, printer, and calculator.
> You will need the following items:
>   1. Computer
>   2. Printer
>   3. Calculator
> You will need the following items: (1) typewriter, (2) equipment, and (3) stationery.

Sometimes the words *the following* do not introduce the list or example. Instead the sentence implies that you are going to list or give an example or explanation.

> Three items were needed: computer, printer, and calculator.
> The pickup truck was large enough for these items: refrigerator, stove, and dishwasher.
> He has three children: Carl, Jesse, and Elaine.
> His smile was for one reason: He had won first prize.

Note Don't confuse a listing with a series. *The following* is not implied in a series.

> Joe loaded the plates, cups, and saucers into the dishwasher.
> They sent food, clothing, and medicine.
> Jan loaded the dishwasher with plates, cups, and saucers.
> I would like to travel to Seattle, Portland, and Tacoma.

CHECKPOINT 6-1

YOUR GOAL: Get 9 or more sentences correct.

In the following sentences, insert colons in the proper place. The first sentence has been completed as an example.

- Diana asked her sister to buy the following items: milk, eggs, meat, vegetables, and bread.

1. She will need the following tools in her job a wrench, saw, pliers, screwdriver, and hammer.

2. Three neighbors work for the highway department Jack, Claudia, and Quyen.

Unit 6 Colon and Semicolon

3. Last year they visited the following three states Florida, Georgia, and Alabama.

4. He has four children Marie, Tina, Nick, and Josh.

5. They ordered tacos, burritos, corn chips, and fajitas.

6. The restaurant will provide the following items plates, cups, forks, and spoons.

7. The meetings will be held in St. Paul, Madison, and Milwaukee.

8. She received the following gifts a TV, a camera, and a dress.

9. He visited the following cities Dallas, Fort Worth, Oklahoma City, and Tulsa.

10. She sorted the following coins in the cash drawer quarters, dimes, nickels, and pennies.

☞ **Check your work on page 80. Record your score on page 83.**

Sometimes you may want to introduce one complete thought or phrase. This helps the reader to better understand what you want to say.

Then came the opportunity for John to win: He had the winning lotto card.
My reason is simple: I ran out of gasoline.

Between Hours and Minutes

Rule Use a colon to separate the hour and minutes when expressing time.

When a colon separates the hour and minutes, no space is placed before or after the colon.

8:30 a.m.   5:45 p.m.

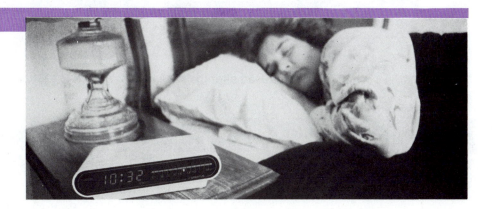

Illustration 6-2

The colon flashes on Judy's alarm clock between the hour and the minutes.

> **DID YOU KNOW?**
>
> The abbreviation a.m. means before noon. This is the time from midnight to noon. It comes from the Latin *ante meridiem* which means before noon.
>
> The abbreviation p.m. means after noon. This is the time from noon to midnight. It comes from the Latin *post meridiem* which means after noon.

In Business Salutations

Rule A colon may be used after the salutation of a business letter.

   Dear Ms. Gee: Dear Dr. Alvarez:

Note A comma is used after the salutation of a personal or friendly letter.

   Dear Ed,   Dear Denise,

```
Dear Ms. Gee:

In regard to your recent letter, please be
assured that we intend to ship your order as
soon as we can.  We value you as a customer,
and we certainly appreciate your patience.
Please accept my apologies for the delay.

Sincerely,


Alan Singleton
President
```

Illustration 6-3

A colon may be used after the salutation of a business letter.

CHECKPOINT 6–2

YOUR GOAL: Get 5 correct.

Insert the colon or comma in the proper place. The first sentence has been completed as an example.

Unit 6   Colon and Semicolon

- He goes to work at 6:45 a.m.

1. The meeting will begin at 1 45 p.m. on Tuesday.
2. He will leave home at 2 15 p.m.
3. Punctuation for the salutation to a business letter
   `Dear Mr. Mendoza`
4. Punctuation for the salutation to a personal letter
   `Dear Mary`
5. The movie begins at 7 30 p.m.

☞ **Check your work on page 80. Record your score on page 83.**

THE SEMICOLON

The semicolon (;) is a mark that joins two complete thoughts. It is not used to introduce or to end a sentence. The semicolon helps you to move from one complete thought to the next one.

Between Two Complete Thoughts

The semicolon shows that the two complete thoughts have equal weight. The sentence is balanced on both sides. Both independent clauses have a subject and a predicate.

Rule Use a semicolon to join two closely related complete thoughts in a compound sentence when connecting words are omitted. Connecting words are *and, but, or,* and *nor.* Connecting words are also called *conjunctions.*

> Daryl sleeps late on Saturday; this is his day off.
> Judy sleeps late on Friday; she works the Thursday night shift at the hospital.
> The driving conditions were poor; the snow continued to blow and drift.

Before Connecting Words

Two complete thoughts often join connecting words: *and, but,* and *or.* In Unit 3 you learned that you use a comma before connecting words in compound sentences.

> He decided to move to Denton, *and* she moved to Tulsa.

Rule Use a semicolon to join two independent clauses when one or both clauses have a comma, and confusion might result if a comma joined the clauses.

Unit 6   Colon and Semicolon

DID YOU KNOW?

You have learned that you may choose different ways to separate or join complete thoughts. Using different ways adds variety to your writing and enables the reader to better understand what you are trying to say.

1. Separate complete thoughts with a period.

   Joyce works during the day at the bank.
   Jorge works the night shift at the shoe factory.

2. Join two related complete thoughts with connecting words such as *and*, *but*, *or*, *for* with a comma.

   Joyce works the day shift at the bank, and Jorge works the night shift at the shoe factory.

3. Join two complete thoughts that are closely related with a semicolon.

   Joyce works during the day at the bank; Jorge works the night shift at the shoe factory.
   Dimitri goes to the learning center early in the morning; this is his best time to work on the computer.

   Why would you choose to use a semicolon to join clauses? Perhaps you have too many short sentences in your writing. There may be too many long pauses or breaks between sentences. A semicolon is a longer pause than a comma; a semicolon is a shorter pause than a period.

Confusing: Our letter stated that we wanted oranges, apples, bananas, tomatoes, and lemons, and they sent us 10 bushels of potatoes.

Better: Our letter stated that we needed oranges, apples, bananas, tomatoes, and lemons; and they sent us 10 bushels of potatoes.

If the compound sentence is easy to read, use a comma to join the two clauses.

He decided to move to Denton, Texas, and she moved to Tulsa, Oklahoma.

CHECKPOINT 6–3

YOUR GOAL: Get 9 or more correct.

Read the sentences and insert either a semicolon or comma in the proper place. The first sentence has been completed as an example.

- Juanita is late for school; George is on his way.

1. She cleared the table Flo brought the main dish.

Unit 6   Colon and Semicolon   59

2. Keyboarding speed does not come easily it requires practice.

3. The program begins today but I do not know the time.

4. The program begins today I do not know the time.

5. Keyboarding speed is important accuracy is also important.

6. Jody wants to go to school to study computers but she needs to work to pay for her expenses.

7. Bowling is not just exercise it is also Bob's favorite hobby.

8. Jim will go to the ball game but he will stop by the office on the way home.

9. Uncle Matt coaches a soccer team he also works with the Boy Scouts.

10. Uncle Matt coaches a soccer team and he also works with the Boy Scouts.

☞ **Check your work on page 80. Record your score on page 83.**

Between Transitional Words and Phrases

Sometimes you may want to join complete thoughts with transitional words. When you are "in transition," you are moving from one place to another. Transitional words help you to move from one complete thought to the next complete thought.

Rule   Use a semicolon between complete thoughts that are joined by transitional words or phrases. Place a comma after the transitional expression. Transitional words are italicized in the following sentences:

Little Fay usually likes hamburgers; *however*, this evening she would rather have pizza.
They really liked the movie; *therefore*, they told their friends about it.
Jackie wrote down a list of things she needed; *for example*, she needed furniture, dishes, and a rug.

Transitional Expressions

accordingly	meanwhile
consequently	moreover
for example	nevertheless
furthermore	on the other hand
however	that is
in addition	therefore

Unit 6 Colon and Semicolon

DID YOU KNOW?

Transitional words help your writing to move smoothly. When you are in transition, you are moving. You may be in transition from school to work. You may also be in transition from one job to another job. The word *transition* comes from the Latin word *transire,* meaning to go across. A transient is a person who moves from one place to another. If you are in transit, you are moving. Many bus companies are called "transit companies."

CHECKPOINT 6–4

YOUR GOAL: Get 4 or more correct.

In the space provided, rewrite each of the pairs of sentences to form one sentence using a semicolon. The first sentence has been completed as an example.

- Charles was tired after practice. Nevertheless, he agreed to help his father with yard work.

  Charles was tired after practice; nevertheless, he agreed to help his father with yard work.

1. August was a hot month. On the other hand, so was July.

2. Jenny went to St. Paul, Minnesota, for vacation. However, she came home after one day.

3. Everyone thought the movie was good. Furthermore, they decided to recommend it to their friends.

4. Eduardo is proud of his school work. For example he earned the highest grade in English.

Unit 6 Colon and Semicolon

5. If you ask for advice, I'll give it. However, you will not like what I'm going to say.

_____

_____

 Check your work on page 80. Record your score on page 83.

Between Items in a Series

Usually commas separate items in a series. Sometimes you will use semicolons in a series.

Rule Use a semicolon to separate groups of words in a series that already contains commas.

> They drove to Denver, Colorado; Santa Fe, New Mexico; and Phoenix, Arizona.
> Several persons attended the builders' meeting: Joe Medina, a bricklayer from Dallas; Marcie James, a carpenter from Tulsa; and Kim Quyen, a plumber from Fort Worth.

CHECKPOINT 6–5

YOUR GOAL: Get 4 or more correct.

Proofread the sentences and insert colons and semicolons in the proper places. The first one has been completed as an example.

- The following people will take the training course: Janet Bates, computer operator; David Robb, secretary; and Pat Goldman, receptionist.

1. Three workers took the keyboarding course Pam Padilla manager Duane Kirby truck driver and Roberta Robins sales clerk.

2. The following relatives attended the wedding Uncle Ben from Chicago Illinois Aunt May from Madison Wisconsin and Aunt Jamie from Davenport Iowa.

3. They hope to visit the following cities on the way Greeley Colorado Wichita Kansas and Kansas City Missouri.

4. The following three items were ordered TV set TV Stock No. 14 CD player CD Stock No. 18 and Video player VCR Stock No. 55.

5. The next regional meetings will be held in the following locations Room 155 Baylor Elementary School Room 243 Medina Middle School and Room 555 Jackson Community College.

 Check your work on page 80. Record your score on page 83.

WHAT YOU HAVE LEARNED

As a result of completing this unit, you have learned to:
- Use a colon to introduce a list of items, an example, or an explanation.
- Use a colon to separate hour and minutes.
- Punctuate the salutation of a business letter using a colon.
- Correctly use a semicolon to join clauses in a compound sentence.
- Use a semicolon before transitional words or phrases in a compound sentence.
- Use a semicolon between items in a series.

PUTTING IT TOGETHER

ACTIVITY 6-1 YOUR GOAL: Get 9 or more sentences correct.

In the following sentences, insert a colon in the proper place. The first sentence has been completed as an example.

- She bought the following items for her young daughter: toy truck, baseball bat, building blocks, and books.

1. He will need the following supplies cotton swabs, scissors, bandages, and aspirin.

2. Three sisters were there Judy, Kim, and Maria.

3. She ordered the following items shovel, hoe, rake, and spade.

4. They will drive through the following states Iowa, Nebraska, and South Dakota.

5. They have three sons Mike, David, and Kevin.

6. The office workers will give their time, money, and hard work.

7. The sales clerk sold the following items two dresses, four shirts, and three pairs of shoes.

8. These people were asked to complete an application Sally Mesten, Gary Nitobe, and Cindy Foote.

9. The three job interviews will be held in the following departments accounting, sales, and transportation.

10. There are job openings in sales, accounting, and transportation.

☞ **Check your work on page 81. Record your score on page 83.**

ACTIVITY 6-2 YOUR GOAL: Get 5 correct.

Rewrite each of the following words and phrases. Insert the missing punctuation. The first one is completed as an example.

- 7 30 a m   7:30 a.m.

1. Dear Miss Ortiz (business letter) _____

2. Dear Rick (personal letter) _____

3. 3 15 p m _____

63

4. 5 02 a m

5. `Dear Mr. Tran`
   (business letter)

☞ **Check your work on page 81. Record your score on page 83.**

ACTIVITY 6-3 YOUR GOAL: Get 4 or more correct.

Combine the following pairs of sentences to form one sentence using a semicolon. The first one has been completed as an example.

- Joe worked hard on the farm all day. Nevertheless, he worked at night cleaning house and preparing meals for the family.

  > Joe worked hard on the farm all day; nevertheless, he worked hard at night cleaning house and preparing meals for the family.

1. A few calves were shipped to the feedlot today. However, many lambs arrived.

2. The motorcycles were delivered to the dock today. Moreover, they arrived in time for the shipment to Brazil.

3. There are many books at the library to read. They need to be checked out.

4. The water was high. Consequently, the bridge was closed.

5. The rain started before noon. It ruined our plans for a family picnic.

☞ **Check your work on page 81. Record your score on page 83.**

Unit 6   Colon and Semicolon

ACTIVITY 6-4 YOUR GOAL: Get 4 or more correct.

Read the following sentences carefully. Then add colons, semicolons, and commas in the proper places. The first one has been completed as an example.

- The following neighbors work for the company: Joyce Chavez, manager; Edith Warren, computer repair person; and Jerry Devlin, sales clerk.

1. Three persons are ready for better jobs Jane Cordova nursing assistant Jack True custodian and David Chu cashier.

2. The following persons will be moving here to work at the new plant Abe Williams Columbus Ohio Enid Sullivan Erie Pennsylvania and Janet Katina Des Moines Iowa.

3. They have worked in plants located in the following cities Santa Fe New Mexico Tucson Arizona and El Paso Texas.

4. They delivered the following goods to the warehouse CD players TV sets stoves and washing machines.

5. He made a soup that included the following items beans garlic carrots celery onions and water.

☞ Check your work on page 81. Record your score on page 83.

ACTIVITY 6-5 YOUR GOAL: Get 4 or more correct.

Read the following sentences carefully. Then add commas or semicolons in the proper places. The first one has been completed as an example.

- Installing carpets requires skill; it also requires practice.

1. She will paint the house on Tuesday but I am not sure what time she will begin.

2. He will repair the kitchen light the apartment manager will pay for it.

3. She will harvest the corn in addition he will deliver the crops to the grain elevator.

4. It snowed in January and February however the biggest snow was in March.

5. Jason headed for Fargo North Dakota but the roads were closed after the blizzard.

☞ Check your work on page 81. Record your score on page 83.

CHECKING WHAT YOU LEARNED

Take this test after completing PUNCTUATION. The test will show you how well you can use punctuation marks and the skills you should improve. When you finish, check your answers. Give yourself 2 points for each correct answer. Record you score on your Personal Progress Record on page 84. The evaluation chart will tell you where you may need additional study.

INSTRUCTIONS: Select the sentence that is correctly punctuated. Place the letter of the correct answer in the blank.

- __a__ 0. (a) They sent a letter to Ms. W. T. Dale.
  - (b) They sent a letter to Ms W T Dale.

Unit 1

_____ 1. (a) John James, Jr., is the manager.
  (b) John James, Jr, is the manager.

_____ 2. (a) Where is the parking lot.
  (b) Where is the parking lot?

_____ 3. (a) Will you please deliver the truck next week?
  (b) Will you please deliver the truck next week.

_____ 4. (a) Please send me a copy of your catalog.
  (b) Please send me a copy of your catalog!

Unit 2

_____ 5. (a) He repaired, the porch, painted the kitchen, and installed a new door.
  (b) He repaired the porch, painted the kitchen, and installed a new door.

_____ 6. (a) Her son was born in Jackson, Mississippi last year.
  (b) Her son was born in Jackson, Mississippi, last year.

_____ 7. (a) The office is located at 403 Park Lane, Houston, TX, 77042-4949.
  (b) The office is located at 403 Park Lane, Houston, TX 77042-4949.

_____ 8. (a) The last family reunion was on April 2, 1991, in Mobile, Alabama.
  (b) The last family reunion was on April 2 1991 in Mobile, Alabama.

Unit 3

_____ 9. (a) Jack is delivering vegetables to stores and Marcia is working in the warehouse.
  (b) Jack is delivering vegetables to stores, and Marcia is working in the warehouse.

66   PUNCTUATION

Checking What You Learned

_____ 10. (a) Joyce loaded the truck, and drove to town to pick up the tires.
(b) Joyce loaded the truck and drove to town to pick up the tires.
_____ 11. (a) Sue and Joe picked up the children and took them on a picnic.
(b) Sue and Joe picked up the children, and took them on a picnic.
_____ 12. (a) David unloaded the furniture and Kim installed the kitchen appliances.
(b) David unloaded the furniture, and Kim installed the kitchen appliances.

Unit 4

_____ 13. (a) In conclusion, we hope that you will enroll in our computer program.
(b) In conclusion we hope that you will enroll in our computer program.
_____ 14. (a) If you learn how to use, punctuation marks correctly your writing will improve.
(b) If you learn how to use punctuation marks correctly, your writing will improve.
_____ 15. (a) The line was busy, when the manager called.
(b) The line was busy when the manager called.
_____ 16. (a) Your order, of course will be sent as soon as possible.
(b) Your order, of course, will be sent as soon as possible.
_____ 17. (a) Joanie Arnett who has repaired computers for five years will fix your printer.
(b) Joanie Arnett, who has repaired computers for five years, will fix your printer.
_____ 18. (a) Ruth Grimes the restaurant manager is moving next month.
(b) Ruth Grimes, the restaurant manager, is moving next month.
_____ 19. (a) We look forward to hearing from you Joe.
(b) We look forward to hearing from you, Joe.

Unit 5

_____ 20. (a) You're invited to the meeting.
(b) Your invited to the meeting.
_____ 21. (a) He placed the pencil on Marys' desk.
(b) He placed the pencil on Mary's desk.
_____ 22. (a) They demanded that all of the hotel workers' wages be increased.
(b) They demanded that all of the hotel workers wages be increased.
_____ 23. (a) Jerry and Jason's truck needs a new paint job.
(b) Jerry's and Jason's truck needs a new paint job.
_____ 24. (a) Roy said, "I will be leaving today".
(b) Roy said, "I will be leaving today."
_____ 25. (a) She read the magazine "Working Woman."
(b) She read the magazine <u>Working Woman.</u>

Unit 6

_____ 26. (a) Four neighbors work at the supermarket: Mary, Joe, Adam, and Jean.
　　　　　(b) Four neighbors work at the supermarket Mary, Joe, Adam, and Jean.

_____ 27. Business letter salutation:
　　　　　(a) Dear Ms. James:
　　　　　(b) Dear Ms. James,

_____ 28. (a) Joe called in last night, he will be late for work.
　　　　　(b) Joe called in last night; he will be late for work.

_____ 29. (a) Judy was tired after work nevertheless, she agreed to help her brother cut wood.
　　　　　(b) Judy was tired after work; nevertheless, she agreed to help her brother cut wood.

_____ 30. (a) Three workers were hired last year: Patty Jensen, secretary, Joe James, custodian, and Robbie Jones, sales clerk.
　　　　　(a) Three workers were hired last year: Patty Jensen, secretary; Joe James, custodian; and Robbie Jones, sales clerk.

☞ **Check your answers on page 81. Record your score on page 84.**

GLOSSARY

A

Abbreviation A short way of writing a word. *Sr.* is an abbreviation for *senior*.

Appositive A group of words that gives additional information about a person, place, or thing. If you leave out the appositive, the meaning of the sentence remains the same. Example: Kim Newman, *the office manager,* will call you.

C

Clause A group of related words that contain a subject and a predicate.

Compound Anything that is made by combining parts. Example of a compound word: *airplane*.

Compound Predicate Two or more predicates in the same sentence. The predicates are connected by *and* and *or*. Example: They *washed the car* and *shopped for groceries*.

Compound Sentence A sentence containing two or more independent clauses combined by connecting words such as *and*, *but*, and *or*. Example: *Jane works at a restaurant, but she would rather work on a ranch.*

Compound Subject Two or more subjects in the same sentence. The subjects are connected by *and* and *or*. Example: *Adam and Bob* built the house.

Contraction A short way of writing two words. The apostrophe indicates that there is one or more letters missing. Examples: *aren't, can't, won't*.

D

Direct Quotation The exact words of the speaker or writer.

E

Essential Clause Group of words that explains or describes a person, place or thing in the sentence. The clause is essential to the meaning of the sentence. Sometimes essential clauses are called *restrictive clauses*. Example: The man *who bought the car* is from New York.

I

Independent Clause A group of words that contains a subject and predicate and can stand alone as a complete sentence.

Introductory Clause A clause that comes before the main idea (independent clause) in a sentence. An introductory clause introduces the main idea. Example: *If you can attend,* I'd like your help.

J

Joint Ownership Two or more persons own the same item. Example: He borrowed *Adam and Ann's* car.

N

Nonessential Clause A clause that interrupts the main idea of the sentence. The clause explains or describes a person, place, or thing in the sentence. Such a clause is not necessary to the meaning of the sentence. Sometimes nonessential clauses are called *nonrestrictive clauses*. Example: Jerry Garcia, *who is the manager of the store,* will call you.

Nonessential Words Words that interrupt the meaning of the sentence. Nonessential words are also called *parenthetical expressions*. Example: His sister, *of course,* will also be there.

Nonrestrictive Clause A clause that interrupts the main idea of the sentence. The clause explains or describes a person, place, or thing in the sentence. Such a clause is not necessary to the meaning of the sentence. Sometimes nonrestrictive clauses are called *nonessential clauses*. Example: Jerry Garcia, *who is the manager of the store,* will call you.

Noun A word that names a person, place, or thing.

P

Parenthetical Expression Words that

interrupt the meaning of the sentence. Parenthetical expressions are also called *nonessential words*. Example: His sister, *of course,* will also be there.

Phrase A short group of related words that does not contain a subject and a predicate.

Possession Ownership.

Predicate The part of the sentence that tells what the subject of a sentence is or does. The predicate contains the verb and its modifiers (words that describe the verb). Example: Jane *washed her car.*

Pronoun A word used in place of a noun. Example: *he, she, they.*

R

Restrictive Clause A group of words that explains or describes a person, place or thing in the sentence. The clause is essential to the meaning of the sentence. Sometimes restrictive clauses are called *essential clauses*. Example: The man *who bought the car* is from New York.

S

Sentence A group of words that expresses a complete thought.

Series three or more similar words or groups of words. Items in a series are placed one after another in a sentence. Example: She will work *Monday, Tuesday,* or *Wednesday.*

Simple Sentence A sentence that has one main idea.

Subject A main word or group of words that tells who or what the sentence is about. The subject may be a single word called a noun. Example: *The boy* threw the ball.

INDEX

A

A.M.:
  defined, 56
  use of periods in, 2
Abbreviations:
  of names of organizations, 3
  of state, when using ZIP code, 11
  of title before or after name, 2
  use of period with, 2–3
Address (direct), use of comma with, 34–35
Address (letter):
  abbreviations in, 2
  commas in, 11–12
  parts of, 11
  street address in, 2, 11
Apostrophe, 40–47, 49–52
  in contractions, 40–41
  to show possession, 42–47
Appositives, 34

B

Balance scales, 21–22
Book titles:
  capitalization in, 49
  underlining of, 49
Business letter:
  address of, 2, 11–12
  salutation (greeting) in, 56–57
But. *See* Connecting words

C

Capitalization:
  in book titles, 49
  in magazine titles, 49
Chapter titles, quotation marks for, 48–49
City, as part of address, 11
Clauses:
  complete. *See* Clauses, independent
  dependent, 29–30
  independent, 21, 57
  introductory, 29–30
  nonessential, 32–34
  nonrestrictive, 33–34
  use of commas with, 21, 29–30, 32–34
  use of semicolons to join, 57
Colon, 53–57, 62–65
  after business salutations, 57
  between hours and minutes, 55–56
  to introduce complete thought or phrase, 55
  after list of items, 54–55
  after salutation (greeting) in business letter, 56–57
  spacing after, 53
Comics, exclamation points in, 5
Comma:
  in addresses, 2, 11–12
  to connect complete thoughts, 16–26
  before connecting words, 9, 21
  with days of the week, 13
  with direct address, 34–35
  before direct quotations, 47–48
  Greek origin of, 11
  between independent clauses, 21
  after introductory clauses, 29–30
  after introductory words and phrases, 28–29
  purpose of, 9
  after salutation of personal letter, 56–57
  to separate items in a series, 9–11
  to separate parts of addresses and dates, 11–13
  to set off appositives, 34
  to set off dependent clauses, 29–30
  to set off interrupting words and phrases, 30–35
  to set off nonessential clauses, 32–34
Command (sentence), 2
  you as understood subject of, 17
Complete thoughts, semicolon to join, 57–59
Compound, defined, 20
Compound sentences:
  punctuating, 22–23
  recognizing, 21–22
  use of semicolon in, 57
Compound subjects and predicates, 19–20
Compound words, 21
Connecting words:
  comma before, 9, 21
  between independent clauses, 21
  in items in a series, 9
  semicolon before, 57–59
Contract, 41
Contractions, 40–41

71

Contractor, 41

D

Dates, 13
Days of the week:
    abbreviation of, 2
    comma after, 13
    spelling out, 2
Dependent clause, 29–30
Direct address, 34–35
Direct question, 4
Direct quotation, 47–48
    comma before, 47–48
    quotation marks for, 47–48
Divided quotations, quotation marks for, 48

E

Ending punctuation marks, 1–8
    exclamation point, 5–8
    period, 2–4, 6–8
    question mark, 2–5, 6–8
Exclamation point, 5–8
    avoiding overuse of, 5
    in comics, 5
    for emphasis, 5
Expressions, parenthetical, 31

G

Greeting, in letter. *See* Salutation

H

Hours and minutes, use of colon to separate, 55–56

I

Independent clauses:
    comma between, 21
    use of semicolon to join, 57–59
Indirect question, 4
Indirect quotation, 47
Initials, in person's name, use of period after, 2
Interrupting words and phrases:
    examples of, 31
    set off by commas, 31–35
Introductory clauses, comma after, 29–30
Introductory thought, word, or phrase:
    colon after, 55
    comma after, 28–29
Items in a series. *See* Series

J

Joint owners, possessive form for, 45–46

L

Language, sign, 5
Letters:
    business, 56–57
    personal, 56–57
Letters of alphabet, omitted, use of apostrophe to indicate, 40–41
List of items:
    colon after, 54
    series differentiated from, 54

M

Magazine articles, titles of, 48–49
Magazine titles:
    capitalization of, 49
    underlining of, 49
Main idea of sentence, 28. *See also* Independent clauses
Months of the year:
    abbreviation of, 2
    spelling out, 2

N

Names:
    abbreviations in or of, 2
    of days and months, 2
    initials of, 2
    as part of address, 11
    titles with, 2
Newspaper articles, titles of, 48–49
Nonessential clauses, use of comma with, 32–34
Nonessential words and phrases:
    examples of, 31
    set off by commas, 31–32
Nonrestrictive clauses, use of comma with, 32–34
Nor. *See* Connecting words
Nouns:
    plural, 44–46
    singular, 42–43

O

Index

OK (O.K., okay), origin of, 3
Omitted letters, use of apostrophe to indicate, 40–41
Or. *See* Connecting words
Owners, joint, 45–46

P

P.M.:
  defined, 56
  use of periods with, 2
Parenthetical expressions, 31
Parts of complete works, use of quotation marks for, 48–49
Period, 2–4, 6–8
  with abbreviations, 2–3
  at end of sentence, 2
  Greek origin of, 4
  after indirect question, 4
  after initials of person's name, 2
  with names of days and months, 2
  in street addresses, 2
  after time periods, 2
Periods of time. *See* Time periods
Personal letters, salutations in, 56–57
Phrases:
  colons with, 55
  commas with, 28–29, 31–35
  defined, 28
  interrupting, 31–35
  introductory, 28–29, 55
  nonessential, 31–32
  semicolons with, 59–61
  transitional, 59–61
Plural nouns, possessive form of, 44–46
Poem titles, quotation marks for, 48–49
Polite request (sentence), 2
  you as subject in, 17
Possession, use of apostrophe to show, 42–47
  with plural nouns, 44–46
  with singular nouns, 42–43
  with two or more persons, 45–46
Possessive pronouns and, 46–47
Predicates:
  compound, 19–20
  simple, 16–17
Pronouns:
  possessive, 46–47
  use of, with contractions, 41
Punctuation, 1–65
  apostrophe, 40–47, 49–52
  colon, 53–57, 62–65
  commas, 9–39
  ending punctuation marks, 1–8
  exclamation point, 5–8
  introduction to, 1–2
  period, 2–4, 6–8
  question mark, 4–5, 6–8
  quotation marks, 47–52
  semicolon, 57–65

Q

Question:
  direct, question mark after, 4
  indirect, period after, 4
Question mark, 4–5, 6–8
Quotation:
  capitalization in a, 72–73
  direct, 47–48
  divided, 48
  indirect, 47
Quotation marks, 47–52
  for direct quotations, 47–48
  for divided quotations, 48
  for parts of complete works, 48–49
  for titles of short works, 48–49

R

Request, as sentence, 2

S

Salutation:
  colon after, in business letter, 56–57
  comma after, in personal letter, 56–57
Semicolon, 57–65
  before connecting words, 57–59
  between independent clauses, 57
  between items in a series, 61
  before transitional words and phrases, 59–61
  between two complete thoughts, 57
Sentence:
  command, 2, 17
  introductory words in, comma after, 28
  period at end of, 2
  polite request, 2
  request, 4
  statement, 2
  compound, 21–23, 57

compound, use of semicolon in, 57
simple, 16–20
Series, items in a:
comma between, 9–11
differentiated from list of items, 54
semicolon between, 61
Short poems, titles of, 48–49
Short stories, titles of, 48–49
Sign language, 5
Signals, commas as, 9
Signs:
abbreviations on,
place names on,
Simple sentences, 16–20
Simple subjects and predicates, 16–17
Singular nouns, possessive form of, 42–43
Spacing, after colon, 53
State, as part of address, 11
Statement, as sentence, 2
Street address:
abbreviation and, 2
commas in, 11
Subjects and predicates:
compound, 19–20
simple, 16–17

T

Thoughts:
introductory, colon after, 55
two complete, semicolon between, 57
Time periods:
A.M. and P.M., 4, 56
days of the week, 2, 13
hours and minutes, use of colon between, 55–56
months of the year, 2
period after, 2
Titles:
of books, magazines, and newspapers, 49
of parts of complete works, 48–49
of short works, 48–49
underlining of, 49
use of quotation marks for, 48–49
Transition, defined, 60
Transitional words and phrases:
examples of, 59
use of semicolon before, 59–61

U

Underlining, of book and magazine titles, 49
Unfortunately, use of comma with, 31

W

Word(s):
abbreviated, 2–3
capitalization of. *See* Capitalization
connecting, 9, 21, 57–59
interrupting, 30–35
introductory, 27–29
nonessential, 31–32
transitional, 59–61

Y

Year:
comma after, 13
comma between date and, 13
months of the, 2
You, as understood subject, 17

Z

ZIP (Zone Improvement Plan) Code, 11

ANSWERS

✓ CHECKING WHAT YOU KNOW

Unit 1	Page
1. b	2
2. a	2
3. b	2
4. a	2

Unit 2	Page
5. b	9
6. a	11
7. b	11
8. b	13

Unit 3	Page
9. a	21
10. a	20
11. a	21
12. a	21

Unit 4	Page
13. b	28
14. a	29
15. b	30
16. a	31
17. a	33
18. b	34
19. a	35

Unit 5	Page
20. b	41
21. b	42
22. b	44
23. b	45
24. a	48
25. a	49

Unit 6	Page
26. a	54
27. a	56
28. b	57
29. a	59
30. b	61

UNIT 1

CHECKPOINT 1–1, PAGE 3

1. truck.
2. Mrs. R. S. Barnes.
3. Dr. Chris Canfield.
4. 7:30 a.m.
5. VCR set.
6. Apt. 202, 110 Main Street.
7. Mary Meza, M.D.
8. Alan Davis, Jr., and Jake Jones, Sr.
9. TV set.
10. letter.

CHECKPOINT 1–2, PAGE 4

1. coming.
2. questions?
3. green.
4. blue?
5. home?

CHECKPOINT 1–3, PAGE 6

1. surprised!
2. Hurry! fire!
   Hurry! fire.
3. Help! accident!
   Help! accident.
4. Oh! flat!
   Oh! flat.
5. down! slippery!
   down! slippery.

ACTIVITY 1–1, PAGE 7

1. year?
2. better.
3. library.
4. bed.
5. babysitter.
6. day.
7. Congratulations! prize!
   Congratulations! prize.
8. 3:30 p.m.
9. Mary Chavez, M.D.
10. 8 p.m. Tuesdays.

ACTIVITY 1–2, PAGE 7

1. open?
2. construction?
3. located.
4. interview?
5. was.
6. meeting?
7. test?
8. test.
9. classroom.
10. name?

ACTIVITY 1–3, PAGE 8

1. tomorrow?
2. center.

75

3. sink?
4. Mr. A. C. Jackson, Jr.
5. car.
6. out! slick!
   out! slick.
7. 6 a.m.
8. Sanchez, M.D.
9. offered.
10. open?
11. blue.
12. arrive.
13. begin?
14. 7:15 p.m.
15. truck.
16. lunch.
17. soup.
18. sandwich.
19. bread?
20. lunch.

UNIT 2

CHECKPOINT 2–1, PAGE 10

1. Billy, Mike, Sue, and
2. center, the pharmacy, store, and
3. Monday, Wednesday, Thursday, and
4. Iowa, Nebraska, South Dakota, and
5. carpenter, plumber, electrician, or
6. No commas needed.
7. June, July, August, or
8. baseball, basketball, swimming, and
9. tire, battery, plugs, and
10. a blueprint, the table, and
11. floor, sheets, and
12. No commas needed.

CHECKPOINT 2–2, PAGE 12

1. Dallas,
2. 102 School Street, Ness City,
3. Boise, Idaho,
4. Apt. 5, 405 Fifth Street, St. Paul,
5. Estes Park, Colorado,
6. Phoenix, Arizona,
7. Las Vegas,
8. Helena,
9. 112 Park Place, Madison,
10. 104 Park Drive, Lansing,

CHECKPOINT 2–3, PAGE 13

1. Tuesday, April 23, 1991,
2. May 1, 1990,
3. May 10, 1995,
4. No commas needed.
5. No commas needed.
6. August 10, 1976,
7. Thursday, December 12
8. June 17, 1990
9. No commas needed.
10. February 6, 1968

ACTIVITY 2–1, PAGE 14

1. nails, lumber, electrical wire, and
2. carpenters, plumbers, electricians, and
3. No commas needed.
4. No commas needed.
5. bakeries, grocery stores,
6. takes out the trash, cleans the floors, scrubs the walls,
7. No commas needed.
8. wheat, barley, and
9. cattle, sheep, and
10. No commas needed.

ACTIVITY 2–2, PAGE 14

1. Santa Barbara,
2. 3720 James Street, Topeka,
3. Salt Lake City, Utah,
4. Apt. 7, 709 Jay Avenue, Madison,
5. Tulsa, Oklahoma,
6. Memphis, Tennessee,
7. Baltimore,
8. Pierre,
9. 402 Jason Court, Cheyenne,
10. Portland,

ACTIVITY 2–3, PAGE 15

1. May 1, 1989, in Mobile,
2. January 1, 1990, in Miami, Florida,
3. Wednesday, September 5, 1998, in Atlanta, Georgia,
4. Apt. 5, 800 Rand Road, Omaha,
5. October 4,

UNIT 3

CHECKPOINT 3–1, PAGE 18

1. <u>The young girl</u>
2. <u>He</u>
3. <u>You</u>
4. <u>The mechanic</u>
5. <u>Ben</u>

CHECKPOINT 3–2, PAGE 19

1. <u>The repair person</u> <u>fixed the computer</u>.
2. <u>Joe</u> <u>studied his lesson</u>.

Answers

3. Send me the bill. you
4. Barbara fixed the car.
5. The leader of the group spoke.
6. Please repair the leaky sink. you
7. He played softball after work.
8. Is Dan selling his bike?
9. My boss called this morning.
10. Kevin walked home.

CHECKPOINT 3–3, PAGE 20

1. She prepared the salad and set the table.
2. You and I will mix the cement.
3. Harold fixed the fence and repaired the tractor.
4. Josie loaded the truck and drove to the ranch.
5. Miners and equipment operators worked at night.
6. Carl and Maria will load the bricks.
7. Joe and Jake cut the wood.
8. Aunt May wrote a letter and called on the phone.
9. Nancy answered the telephone and took a message.
10. Gary climbed the fence and chased the dogs.

CHECKPOINT 3–4, PAGE 22

1. They need to fix the car, or Mary will have to walk.
2. The neighbor's dog barked, but they did not hear it.
3. Jake unloaded the truck, and Joe then sent him to the warehouse.
4. Jane loaded the wheat on the truck, and Joe took it to the grain elevator.
5. The children ride the bus to school, but they still need a ride to football games at night.

CHECKPOINT 3–5, PAGE 22

1. yet,
2. No comma needed.
3. week,
4. No comma needed.
5. groceries,
6. No comma needed.
7. day,
8. week,
9. No comma needed.
10. application,

ACTIVITY 3-1, PAGE 24

1. His brother and sister
2. the teacher
3. Mary and Adam
4. You
5. She
6. You
7. Danny and Pat
8. Jarvis and Kim
9. Diane
10. Her mother

ACTIVITY 3–2, PAGE 24

1. She changed the flat tire.
2. Has he paid the rent?
3. The dog barked.
4. The boy chased the dog.
5. They cleared the table and loaded the dishwasher.
6. Please clean your room and take out the trash.
7. Margaret installed the dishwasher.
8. He washed and ironed the clothes.
9. Jerry rode the horse.
10. Joan cut the wood and loaded the truck.

ACTIVITY 3–3, PAGE 25

1. S   6. C
2. C   7. S
3. S   8. S
4. C   9. C
5. S   10. S

ACTIVITY 3–4, PAGE 25

1. yesterday,
2. No comma needed.
3. week,
4. No comma needed.
5. No comma needed.
6. station,
7. school,
8. No comma needed.
9. waitress,
10. No comma needed.
11. tractor,
12. accident,
13. night,
14. No comma needed.
15. warehouse,

16. dog,
17. doctor,
18. No comma needed.
19. town,
20. day,

UNIT 4

CHECKPOINT 4–1, PAGE 28

1. Finally,
2. As a result,
3. Therefore,
4. First,
5. However,
6. On the other hand,
7. For example,
8. Also,
9. Fortunately,
10. In addition,

CHECKPOINT 4–2, PAGE 30

1. there,
2. high,
3. cabinets,
4. late,
5. changed,
6. work,
7. ill,
8. town,
9. No comma needed
10. No comma needed

CHECKPOINT 4–3, PAGE 32

1. meeting, of course,
2. family, unfortunately,
3. will, therefore,
4. Chan, by all means,
5. Gina, in my opinion,
6. workers, on the other hand,
7. Painters, of course,
8. crew, however,
9. trip, for example,
10. warnings, of course,

CHECKPOINT 4–4, PAGE 33

1. No comma needed.
2. De la Cruz, who is the electronics technician,
3. Sanjay, the new student in our class,
4. Cheyenne, the capital city of Wyoming,
5. Tsuji, who lives next to our mobile home,
6. No comma needed.
7. Allison, who is Lisa's brother,
8. No comma needed.
9. Simental, who is a police officer,

CHECKPOINT 4–5, PAGE 35

1. Joe Peters, the security guard,
2. Alford, my sister's boy friend,
3. shipment, Mr. Quyen,
4. Castro, a computer expert.
5. Robb, the owner of the company,
6. I hope, Ms. Rollans,
7. Kim,
8. Thompson, the chief of police,
9. Cousins, the school nurse,
10. Bob, the oldest member of the family,

ACTIVITY 4–1, PAGE 37

1. example,
2. hand,
3. Apparently,
4. course,
5. early,
6. No,
7. engine,
8. hard,
9. math,
10. First,
11. speed,
12. addition,
13. town,
14. sheep,
15. corner,
16. dinner,
17. addition,
18. closes,
19. No comma needed.
20. work,

ACTIVITY 4–2, PAGE 38

1. car, which has cost very little to repair,
2. Karen, who was the leader of the group,
3. Carr, the carpet installer,
4. Dave, my neighbor's brother,
5. Maria Beltran, a nursing assistant,
6. Please, Mrs. Downey,
7. Painters, of course,
8. crew, however,
9. trip, for example,

Answers

10. Ellis, who has worked in this office for two days,
11. Park, which is near the highway,
12. Gilkey, who is the new teacher,
13. Building, the largest apartment building in town,
14. Alan,
15. I hope, Mr. Chan,
16. will, of course,
17. Manuel, my neighbor's brother,
18. Please, Mr. Torres, deliver the flowers to the hospital.
19. Josephine Henry, who works at the Shear Design Beauty Salon,
20. me, of course,

ACTIVITY 4–3, PAGE 39

1. Before you interview for a job,
2. Of course, your clothing, jewelry, hair style,
3. jobs, by
4. the way,
5. Consequently,
6. the interview,
7. By all means,
8. No commas needed.
9. the interviewer,
10. discussion begins,
11. a question,
12. clearly, however, In addition,
13. Needless to say,
14. No commas needed.
15. No commas needed.
16. Nevertheless,
17. In conclusion,

UNIT 5

CHECKPOINT 5–1, PAGE 41

1. I'm you'll
2. They'll
3. He's
4. It's
5. We're
6. She'll
7. won't
8. doesn't
9. I've
10. can't

CHECKPOINT 5–2, PAGE 43

1. student's
2. plumber's
3. Dan's
4. Ben's
5. Roberta's

CHECKPOINT 5–3, PAGE 45

1. the carpenters' tools
2. the drivers' cars
3. the workers' computers
4. the soldiers' weapons
5. the drivers' licenses
6. the men's clothing
7. two hours' delay
8. the officers' duties
9. the teachers' books
10. the women's names

CHECKPOINT 5–4, PAGE 47

1. its
2. You're
3. hers
4. It's
5. Carla and Pat's
6. theirs
7. yours
8. ours
9. theirs
10. they're

CHECKPOINT 5–5, PAGE 48

1. "Do . . . keyboard?"
2. No quotation marks.
3. "I will . . . course."
4. "You . . . now."
5. No quotation marks.
6. "I . . . tonight."
7. "I . . . tomorrow,"
8. "I . . . morning."
9. "I hope," "that . . . time."
10. "The . . . dock," "is . . . track."

CHECKPOINT 5–6, PAGE 49

1. "God Bless America"
2. "What's News?"
3. "Time to Buy."
4. "Hearts and Flowers."
5. "Know Your Computer."

ACTIVITY 5–1, PAGE 50

1. aren't
2. Dale's
3. didn't
4. Garcia's

5. I'm
6. today's
7. Let's
8. won't
9. No apostrophe needed.
10. weeks'
11. week's
12. It's
13. ladies'
14. company's
15. workers'
16. shouldn't
17. Kevin's
18. children's
19. No apostrophe needed.
20. you're

ACTIVITY 5–2 PAGE 51

1. "Tips for Parents."
2. "The office . . . floor."
3. No quotation marks needed.
4. "Snowbound."
5. No quotation marks needed.
6. "The next meeting," "will . . . night."
7. "Business Letters."
8. "Best Food Buys."
9. "I . . . school."
10. "The . . . good," "but . . . report."

ACTIVITY 5–3 PAGE 51

1. I'd
2. Aren't
   didn't
   me,
3. "Mom . . . Josie?"
4. "I'm . . . old,"
5. he said, "to . . . reunion."
6. "Families and Memories."
7. I'm
8. We're
   I'm
   Jane's
9. I've
   Jake's
10. said, "If
11. Roberta's new address."
12. asked, "What's happening?"
13. haven't,
14. "I'm . . . address."
15. family's
16. There's
    she'll

17. Marlene's
18. Judy's

UNIT 6

CHECKPOINT 6–1, PAGE 54

1. job:
2. department:
3. states:
4. children:
5. No colon needed.
6. items:
7. No colon needed.
8. gifts:
9. cities:
10. drawer:

CHECKPOINT 6–2, PAGE 56

1. 1:45
2. 2:15
3. Dear Mr. Mendoza:
4. Dear Mary,
5. 7:30

CHECKPOINT 6–3, PAGE 58

1. table;
2. easily;
3. today,
4. today;
5. important;
6. computers,
7. exercise;
8. game,
9. team;
10. team,

CHECKPOINT 6–4, PAGE 60

1. month; on
2. vacation; however,
3. good; furthermore,
4. work; for
5. it; however,

CHECKPOINT 6–5, PAGE 61

1. course: Pam Padilla, manager; Duane Kirby, truck driver; and Roberta Robins, sales clerk.
2. wedding: Uncle Ben from Chicago, Illinois; Aunt May from Madison, Wisconsin; and Aunt Jamie from Davenport, Iowa.
3. way: Greeley, Colorado; Wichita, Kansas; and Kansas City, Missouri.

Answers

4. ordered: TV set, TV Stock No. 14; CD player, CD Stock No. 18; and Video player, VCR Stock No. 55.
5. locations: Room 155, Baylor Elementary School; Room 243, Medina Middle School; and Room 555, Jackson Community College.

ACTIVITY 6–1, PAGE 63

1. supplies:
2. there:
3. items:
4. states:
5. sons:
6. No colon needed.
7. items:
8. application:
9. departments:
10. No colon needed.

ACTIVITY 6–2, PAGE 63

1. Ortiz:
2. Rick,
3. 3:15 p.m.
4. 5:02 a.m.
5. Tran:

ACTIVITY 6–3, PAGE 64

1. today; however,
2. today; moreover,
3. read; they
4. high; consequently,
5. noon; it

ACTIVITY 6–4, PAGE 65

1. jobs: Jane Cordova, nursing assistant; Jack True, custodian; and David Chu, cashier.
2. plant: Abe Williams, Columbus, Ohio; Enid Sullivan, Erie, Pennsylvania; and Janet Katina, Des Moines, Iowa.
3. cities: Santa Fe, New Mexico; Tucson, Arizona; and El Paso, Texas.
4. warehouse: CD players, TV sets, stoves, and washing machines.
5. items: beans, garlic, carrots, celery, onions, and water.

ACTIVITY 6–5, PAGE 65

1. Tuesday, but
2. light; the
3. corn; in addition,
4. February; however,
5. Fargo, North Dakota, but

✓ CHECKING WHAT YOU LEARNED

Unit 1	Page
1. a	2
2. b	2
3. b	2
4. a	2

Unit 2	Page
5. b	9
6. b	11
7. b	11
8. a	13

Unit 3	Page
9. b	21
10. b	20
11. a	21
12. b	21

Unit 4	Page
13. a	28
14. b	29
15. b	30
16. b	31
17. b	33
18. b	34
19. b	35

Unit 5	Page
20. a	41
21. b	42
22. a	44
23. a	45
24. b	48
25. b	49

Unit 6	Page
26. a	54
27. a	56
28. b	57
29. b	59
30. b	61

PERSONAL PROGRESS RECORD

Name: _____

✓ CHECKING WHAT YOU KNOW

Use the chart below to determine the areas you need to do the most work. In the space provided, write the total number of points you got right for each content area. Give yourself 2 points for each correct answer. Then add up the total number of points right to find your final score. Circle those items you answere correctly. As you begin your study, pay close attention to those areas where you missed half or more of the questions.

Content Area	Item Number	Study Pages	Total Points	Number Right
Ending Punctuation Marks	1, 2, 3, 4	1-6	8	
Commas That Separate	5, 6, 7, 8	9-13	8	
Commas That Connect Complete Thoughts	9, 10, 11, 12	16-23	8	
Commas That Set Aside	13, 14, 15, 16, 17, 18, 19	27-26	14	
Apostrophe and Direct Quotations	20, 21, 22, 23, 24, 25	40-48	12	
Colon and Semicolon	26, 27, 28, 29, 30	53-62	10	

Date _____   Total Points: 60   Your Score: ☐

UNIT 1: Ending Punctuation Marks

Exercise	Score
Checkpoint 1-1	_____
Checkpoint 1-2	_____
Checkpoint 1-3	_____
Activity 1-1	_____
Activity 1-2	_____
Activity 1-3	_____
TOTAL	_____

HOW ARE YOU DOING?

74–85	Excellent
71–73	Good
65–70	Fair
Less than 65	See Instructor

Personal Progress Record

UNIT 2: Commas That Separate

Exercise	Score
Checkpoint 2-1	_____
Checkpoint 2-2	_____
Checkpoint 2-3	_____
Activity 2-1	_____
Activity 2-2	_____
Activity 2-3	_____
TOTAL	_____

HOW ARE YOU DOING?
93–106	Excellent
87–92	Good
81–86	Fair
Less than 81	See Instructor

UNIT 3: Commas That Connect Complete Thoughts

Exercise	Score
Checkpoint 3-1	_____
Checkpoint 3-2	_____
Checkpoint 3-3	_____
Checkpoint 3-4	_____
Checkpoint 3-5	_____
Activity 3-1	_____
Activity 3-2	_____
Activity 3-3	_____
Activity 3-4	_____
TOTAL	_____

HOW ARE YOU DOING?
85–95	Excellent
79–84	Good
73–78	Fair
Less than 73	See Instructor

UNIT 4: Commas That Set Aside

Exercise	Score
Checkpoint 4-1	_____
Checkpoint 4-2	_____
Checkpoint 4-3	_____
Checkpoint 4-4	_____
Checkpoint 4-5	_____
Activity 4-1	_____
Activity 4-2	_____
Activity 4-3	_____
TOTAL	_____

HOW ARE YOU DOING?
96–107	Excellent
88–95	Good
80–87	Fair
Less than 80	See Instructor

UNIT 5: Apostrophe and Direct Quotations

Exercise	Score
Checkpoint 5-1	_____
Checkpoint 5-2	_____
Checkpoint 5-3	_____
Checkpoint 5-4	_____
Checkpoint 5-5	_____
Checkpoint 5-6	_____
Activity 5-1	_____
Activity 5-2	_____
Activity 5-3	_____
TOTAL	_____

HOW ARE YOU DOING?
89–98	Excellent
81–88	Good
74–80	Fair
Less than 74	See Instructor

UNIT 6: Colon and Semicolon

Exercise	Score
Checkpoint 6-1	_____
Checkpoint 6-2	_____
Checkpoint 6-3	_____
Checkpoint 6-4	_____
Checkpoint 6-5	_____
Activity 6-1	_____
Activity 6-2	_____
Activity 6-3	_____
Activity 6-4	_____
Activity 6-5	_____
TOTAL	_____

HOW ARE YOU DOING?
57–65	Excellent
53–56	Good
50–52	Fair
Less than 50	See Instructor

Name: _____

✓ CHECKING WHAT YOU LEARNED

Use the chart below to determine the areas you need to do the most work. In the space provided, write the total number of points you got right for each content area. Give yourself 2 points for each correct answer. Then add up the total number of points right to find your final score. Review those areas where you missed half or more of the questions.

Content Area	Item Number	Study Pages	Total Points	Number Right
Ending Punctuation Marks	1, 2, 3, 4	1-6	8	
Commas That Separate	5, 6, 7, 8	9-13	8	
Commas That Connect Complete Thoughts	9, 10, 11, 12	16-23	8	
Commas That Set Aside	13, 14, 15, 16, 17, 18, 19	27-26	14	
Apostrophe and Direct Quotations	20, 21, 22, 23, 24, 25	40-48	12	
Colon and Semicolon	26, 27, 28, 29, 30	53-62	10	

Date _____   Total Points: 60   Your Score: ☐